100 Questions about Sleep and Sleep Disorders

100 Questions about Sleep and Sleep Disorders

By

Sudhansu Chokroverty, MD, FRCP, FACP

Blackwell Science

©2001 by Blackwell Science, Inc.

Editorial Offices:
Commerce Place, 350 Main Street, Malden, Massachusetts 02148, USA
Osney Mead, Oxford OX2 0EL, England
25 John Street, London WC1N 2BL, England
23 Ainslie Place, Edinburgh EH3 6AJ, Scotland
54 University Street, Carlton, Victoria 3053, Australia
Other Editorial Offices:
Blackwell Wissenschafts-Verlag GmbH, Kurfürstendamm 57, 10707 Berlin, Germany
Blackwell Science KK, MG Kodenmacho Building, 7-10 Kodenmacho Nihonbashi, Chuo-ku, Tokyo 104, Japan
Iowa State University Press, A Blackwell Science Company, 2121 S. State Avenue, Ames, Iowa 50014-8300, USA

Distributors:

USA

Blackwell Science, Inc.
Commerce Place
350 Main Street
Malden, Massachusetts 02148
(Telephone orders: 800-215-1000 or 781-388-8250; fax orders: 781-388-8270)

Canada

Login Brothers Book Company
324 Saulteaux Crescent
Winnipeg, Manitoba R3J 3T2
(Telephone orders: 204-837-2987)

Australia

Blackwell Science Pty, Ltd.
54 University Street
Carlton, Victoria 3053
(Telephone orders: 03-9347-0300; fax orders: 03-9349-3016)

Outside North America and Australia

Blackwell Science, Ltd.
c/o Marston Book Services, Ltd.
P.O. Box 269
Abingdon
Oxon OX14 4YN
England
(Telephone orders: 44-01235-465500; fax orders: 44-01235-465555)

Acquisitions: Chris Davis
Development: Julia Casson
Production: Shawn Girsberger
Manufacturing: Lisa Flanagan
Marketing Manager: Anne Stone
Cover design by Leslie Haimes
Interior design by Eve Siegel
Typeset by Best-set Typesetter Ltd., Hong Kong
Printed and bound by Capital City Press

Printed in the United States of America
02 03 04 5 4 3 2

The Blackwell Science logo is a trade mark of Blackwell Science Ltd., registered at the United Kingdom Trade Marks Registry

Library of Congress Cataloging-in-Publication Data
Chokroverty, Sudhansu.
    One hundred questions about sleep and sleep disorders / by Sudhansu Chokroverty.
        p. ; cm.
    Includes bibliographical references and index.
    ISBN 0-86542-583-3 (alk. paper)
    1. Sleep disorders—Miscellanea.   2. Sleep–Miscellanea.   I. Title.
    [DNLM: 1. Sleep Disorders—Examination Questions.   2.
Sleep—physiology—Examination Questions.   WM 18.2 C546o 2001]
    RC547 C483 2001
    616.8′498—dc21

00-052961

Contents

Acknowledgements

It is my great pleasure to express my gratitude and appreciation to my wife, Manisha Chokroverty, MD, for forbearance and unfailing support during preparation of this book and for suggesting some of the questions in this monograph.

I would like to thank Mark Mahowald, MD for reviewing the book and for providing thoughtful and insightful comments.

I would like to thank my assistant Errika Thompson for typing and making revisions. I must thank Christopher Davis, Executive Editor, Medicine, at Blackwell Science, Inc. for his thoughtfulness and professionalism. I should also like to thank Shawn Girsberger and Julia Casson of Blackwell Science, Inc. for their help in publishing the book. Finally, I must thank my numerous patients who, over the years, have taught me the value of listening to them in order to learn real sleep medicine, which cannot be mastered by reading books only.

Introduction

Sleep has fascinated mankind since time immemorial. This interest has been reflected in the writings of the poets, philosophers, and scientists alike. In the second half of the last century, significant developments took place in our understanding of sleep. Public awareness about the importance of a good night's sleep is now increasing, thanks to the efforts of the American Academy of Sleep Medicine, other scientific organizations (such as the Sleep Section of the American Academy of Neurology and the American Thoracic Society), National Sleep Foundation, and print and broadcast media.

Why should we be interested in knowing about sleep? Some fundamental facts about the magnitude of the problem go a long way toward answering this question. According to a National Commission for Sleep Disorders Research (NCSDR) report published in 1993, approximately 40 million Americans suffer from chronic disorders of sleep and wakefulness. The vast majority of these individuals remain undiagnosed and untreated by the medical community, contributing to expenses that are measured in terms of billions of dollars. An additional 20 to 30 million people experience intermittent sleep problems. Several recent surveys have revealed that one-third of Americans suffer from sleeplessness; in 10 percent of these individuals, the problem is a persistent one. The Department of Transportation estimates that 200,000 automobile accidents each year may be sleep-related. In a 1995 Gallup survey, one-third of adults admitted having dozed off while driving a car.

Other startling statistics have been gathered about sleep disorders. For example, an estimated 25 to 30 million Americans suffer from chronic insomnia, and 15 to 20 million suffer from sleep apnea. In an important study from Wisconsin, 4 percent of men and 2 percent of women between 30 and 60 years were found to have sleep apnea. Five million Americans suffer from sleep disorders due to shift work. More than 250,000 Americans have narcolepsy, a disorder of excessive sleepiness.

Several national and international disasters can also be cited to illustrate the magnitude of sleep-related problems. A number of catastrophes are thought to be related to fatigue and sleepiness, including the *Exxon*

Valdes oil spill in Alaska; the near-nuclear disaster at Three Mile Island, Pennsylvania; the nuclear accident at Chernobyl in the former Soviet Union; the Bhopal (India) gas leak disaster, which killed nearly 20,000 people; and the *Challenger* space shuttle disaster.

It is, therefore, imperative for both the public and members of the health care profession to be aware of the importance of a good night's sleep and sleep problems. This book of 100 questions will cover various aspects of normal and abnormal sleep, which are of practical relevance.

1. What is sleep?

Humankind has been asking this question since antiquity. More correctly, it should be stated as "What is trying to get to sleep?" Most of us go to sleep at night (unless we are working a night shift). We finish our day's activities and, after relaxing in the evening, we prepare to go to sleep. We lie down, either on the back or side, close our eyes, and try to forget about the world of wakefulness. Slowly, we begin drifting into a state beyond wakefulness. When we do not see, hear, or perceive things in a rational or logical manner, we are in another world, where we have no control, our brain cannot respond logically and adequately, and our body is relatively immobile. We are now entering into what is termed "predormitum." Soon, we are drifting from lighter to deeper stages of sleep. We are now unconscious. Fortunately, this state is reversible—a characteristic that differentiates sleep from irreversible coma (complete unconsciousness as a result of a disease) and death. We all wake up to see the world of wakefulness after seven to eight hours of sleep.

Sleep is not simply an absence of wakefulness— it is not just a passive phenomenon resulting from withdrawal of all sensory stimuli. Many areas of the brain remain active during sleep.

Sleep is not simply an absence of wakefulness—it is not just a passive phenomenon resulting from withdrawal of all sensory stimuli. Many areas of the brain remain active during sleep. Both passive mechanisms (for example, withdrawal of all external and internal stimulation) and active mechanisms contribute to sleep. All of the mechanisms responsible for generating sleep are located within the brain. Indeed, this function of the brain contributes to the individual's overall health, affecting not only the brain but also the entire body as evidenced by the many diseases resulting from too much sleep, too little sleep, inappropriate timing of sleep, or abnormal movements and behavior intruding into sleep.

Modern sleep scientists define sleep based on the behavior of the person while asleep and the physiological changes that occur in the waking brain electrical rhythms as one is drifting into sleep. The behavioral criteria include a characteristic posture, relative immobility, impaired response to external stimulation, and closed eyes. The physiologic criteria

1

define the various sleep stages and are based on recordings of electrical activities of the brain (electroencephalogram, or EEG), the muscles (electromyogram, or EMG), and eye movement (electro-oculogram, or EOG).

We divide sleep broadly into two states: non-rapid eye movement (NREM) sleep and rapid eye movement (REM) sleep. Thus we exist in three states—wakefulness, NREM, and REM sleep with different controls and functions.

NREM sleep is further divided into four stages. In stage I, the predominant wakeful brain rhythms of an adult decrease to less than half of those seen in the wakeful state, the muscle tone decreases a little, and some rolling, slow eye movements may take place. In stage II NREM sleep, brain electrical activities show a characteristic pattern, called sleep spin-

All of the mechanisms responsible for generating sleep are located within the brain.

dles (rhythms of 14 to 16 cycles per second that are seen in surface recordings taken from the front and center of the head); the sleep spindles are accompanied by slower waves (less than 4 cycles per second) during less than 20 percent of the time. Stages III and IV NREM sleep are grouped together and called slow wave sleep or deep sleep. Waves consisting of fewer than 4 cycles per second appear during 20 to 50 percent of the time in stage III, but account for more than 50 percent of the time spent in stage IV NREM sleep.

Approximately 5 to 10 minutes after sleep onset, we drift from stage I to stage II; in about one hour, we go into slow wave sleep. Roughly 60 to 90 minutes after sleep onset, we enter into the world of dream sleep— that is, REM sleep, as most dreams occur at this stage. Eyeballs move rapidly under the closed eyelids (hence the name "rapid eye movement sleep"). Muscle tone in the EMG recording decreases markedly or is absent, and the brain waves (EEG) resemble those noted during wakefulness. NREM and REM sleep then alternate in a cyclical manner (about four to six cycles) interspersed with brief periods of wakefulness throughout the night. During the first third of the night, slow wave sleep dominates; conversely, during the last third of the night, REM sleep dominates. Most of the time (50 to 55 percent of the sleep period), we stay in stage II NREM sleep. REM sleep accounts for 20 to 25 percent of the sleep period.

The sleep pattern just described is the one seen in a normal adult. Different sleep patterns, including the time occupied by the different stages of sleep, are observed in children and the elderly. For example, newborn infants spend 50 percent of the sleep time in REM sleep and the other 50 percent in NREM sleep. The adult pattern becomes established at approximately ten years of age.

2. Why do we sleep?

If we do not have adequate sleep at night, we feel sleepy and irritable throughout the day. According to some recent evidence, both the brain and the rest of the body need an optimal amount of sleep. Although the exact function of sleep is not known, several theories have been proposed based on the results of animal and human sleep deprivation experiments. For example, we may require sleep for energy conservation and for restoration of the body and brain that allows them to function adequately during the wakeful period. Some evidence suggests that sleep is needed for consolidation of memory and for adequate stimulation of various circuits within the brain that ensure its proper functioning. In addition, sleep may provide for regulation of the body temperature.

Both the brain and the rest of the body need an optimal amount of sleep.

3. What is my sleep requirement?

Human sleep requirements vary depending on a person's age. The average requirement for a normal adult man or woman is approximately eight hours. Sleep requirements, just like many behavioral functions and requirements, assume a bell-shaped curve, however. Thus some people require less than the average amount of sleep and some require more sleep to function adequately during waking hours. Some individuals can get by with six to seven hours of sleep (or less); others require nine to ten hours of sleep at night. The basic sleep requirement is defined by heredity, rather than by any environmental influence.

Human sleep requirements vary depending on a person's age. The average requirement for a normal adult man or woman is approximately eight hours.

4. What happens if I am sleep-deprived?

Sleep deprivation (partial or complete) experiments have been conducted in both human and animals. In rats, complete sleep deprivation lasting for 10 to 30 days caused the animals to lose temperature control and weight despite increase in food intake; eventually, the rats died. In 1965, a 17-year-old California student named Randy Gardner tried to set a world record by staying awake for 264 hours and 12 minutes. He then slept for 14 hours and 40 minutes without any permanent adverse effects. During the sleep deprivation experiment, Gardner was, however, drifting into transient periods of NREM stage I (see question #1) known as microsleep.

Sleep deprivation causes fatigue; sleepiness; deterioration of performance, attention, and motivation; and diminishment of mental concentration and intellectual capacity. It also increases the chances of accidents at work and during driving.

Sleep deprivation causes fatigue; sleepiness; deterioration of performance, attention, and motivation; and diminishment of mental concentration and intellectual capacity. It also increases the chances of accidents at work and during driving. Thus sleep deprivation lowers the quality of life and jeopardizes both personal and public safety. It does not cause permanent damage to the nervous system, however. Nevertheless, sleep deprivation may have been responsible for many national and international catastrophes (as described in the Introduction).

5. Can a person either become sick or die after complete sleep deprivation?

It is impossible, from both ethical and practical standpoints, to completely sleep-deprive a human. During sleep deprivation experiments in humans, researchers have noted the occurrence of frequent periods of "microsleep." Subjects have been found to doze repeatedly with transient periods of stage

I NREM sleep (see question #1), with heaviness or drooping of the eyelids and sagging of the head.

Humans do not suffer from serious mental impairment or permanent nervous system damage following sleep deprivation. In an earlier experiment, subjects who awakened after REM sleep deprivation were thought to experience hallucinations and other psychotic features; these findings could not be replicated in later experiments, however. An increased amount of slow wave and dream (REM) sleep does take place in the recovery period after sleep deprivation.

> *Humans do not suffer from serious mental impairment or permanent nervous system damage following sleep deprivation.*

Animals who are subjected to total sleep deprivation will die. This finding was made by Rechtschaffen and colleagues in their sleep deprivation experiments in rats (see question #4).

6. Why do some people go to sleep earlier and others go to sleep late?

Two distinct groups of individuals exist as defined by their sleep habits. Members of the first group go to sleep late and wake up late in the morning. These people cannot function well early in the day but become energetic in the evening and function best at that time. These individuals are called evening types ("owls"). The members of the other group go to sleep early in the evening and wake up early in the morning. They are energetic and vigorous in the morning but become tired and exhausted in the evening. These individuals are the morning types ("larks"). A person's sleep habits are probably determined genetically rather than by any environmental factor.

> *Two distinct groups of individuals exist as defined by their sleep habits.*

7. How does sunrise or sunset control our sleep-wake habits?

Our sleep-wake habits are controlled not only by external light and darkness as determined by sunrise and sunset, but also by our internal body clock. This question was first raised more than two and a half centuries ago by a French astronomer named de Mairin. He noticed that the leaves of a heliotrope plant would open at sunrise and close at sunset, even when the plant was kept inside away from sunlight. This observation led de Mairin to conclude that an internal clock in the plant must control the opening and closing of the leaves. Only in 1980 did scientists discover the existence of an internal clock in rats. Shortly thereafter, researchers confirmed that such a clock operates in humans as well.

The human internal clock is thought to reside within a cluster of nerve cells (called suprachiasmatic nuclei) located deep in the center of the brain above the pituitary gland, the organ that is responsible for secretion of several important hormones. The paired suprachiasmatic nuclei are part of the hypothalamus, which controls the secretion of the hormones, food and water intake, body temperature, and emotion. These nerve cells are located above the crossing pathways that transmit signals from retina (the layer of nerve cells in the back of the eye responsible for transmitting visual images) to the back of the brain. This internal clock has widespread connections—not only with the retina for receiving light from the outside world, but also with other parts of the nervous system. As a result, it controls the body's sleep-wake cycle, secretion of hormones, and the body's temperature rhythms.

Our sleep-wake habits are controlled not only by external light and darkness as determined by sunrise and sunset, but also by our internal body clock.

Every living cell has a rhythm. For example, our sleep-wake habit follows a circadian (from the Latin *circa,* meaning "about," and *dian,* meaning "day") rhythm. Experiments have been conducted to isolate humans from all external sources of time cues (for example, by having subjects live in bunkers, caves, or a special laboratory environment). In these investigations, the individuals had no idea about sunrise, sunset, light, darkness, time of day, or time for meals. They did not have any clock, telephone, or television. They were allowed to sleep, wake up, and eat whenever they wanted. Under these circumstances (called free running rhythm, because the body's internal clock is not synchronized with the environmental time), the length of the human day appears to be not exactly 24 hours but rather a little longer (close to 25 hours).

When our internal clock is not synchronized with the outside time as shown on a wristwatch or clock, all rhythms (sleep-wake, temperature, and hormone secretion) become desynchronized, which disrupts our normal circadian rhythm. Such disruption is very common in this age of jet travel, when we can quickly cross several time zones. In such a case, the internal body clock does not match with the external clock, which gives time according to sunrise and sunset. This disruption of the circadian rhythm can cause serious sleep disturbances and the undesirable consequences resulting from sleep deprivation (see questions #4 and #5), including adverse physical effects in our body causing jet lag syndrome (see question #75).

Although the body can resynchronize the internal and external rhythms, this procedure takes time. Indeed, the time required varies depending on the number of time zones crossed, the direction of travel, and the age of the individual. Older individuals tend to take a longer time than younger people to resynchronize the two clocks. In addition, it is more difficult to adjust when traveling to the east than to the west. On average, it takes roughly one hour per day to adjust when traveling to the west, but an hour and a half per day when traveling to the east. Some sleep specialists have suggested that administration of melatonin, the hormone secreted by the pineal gland in the deeper part of the center of the brain at night (which inspired melatonin's nickname, "hormone of darkness"), may help adjust our internal and external clocks. If true, consumption of melatonin could help alleviate jet lag symptoms. The jury is still out on this issue, and more studies will be necessary to confirm any link.

8. Why does pain cause sleeplessness?

Many people have difficulty going to sleep or in maintaining sleep throughout the night because of pain. Generally, minor aches and pains do not interfere with sleep. On the other hand, moderate to severe pain (such as cancer pain, pain of arthritis, and neuralgic pain) can very definitely interfere with sleep.

Pain also includes an emotional component—some patients perceive pain more readily than others do. Emotional factors may stimulate the arousing system (wakefulness system) in the brain, which will have adverse effects on sleep. We need to relax, lie down quietly in bed, and forget about everything else in the wakeful world when we are getting ready to go to sleep. Severe pain may cause physical discomfort, lead to repeated shifting of body position, or make us anxious and tense, thereby stimulating the arousing system and causing frequent waking up during the night. All of these factors cause both sleep-onset problems and maintenance insomnia.

In addition to its mechanical and psychological effects (such as anxiety and tension), pain may interact with neurotransmitters (chemicals responsible for transmitting nerve signals) in the brain. These neurotransmitters (for example, adrenaline, noradrenaline, serotonin, and acetycholine) have considerable regulatory influence on sleep-wakefulness. For example, a serotonin deficiency in the brain may reduce the threshold for perception of pain, causing us to feel pain very easily and experience sleep disturbance. In a 1995 Gallup survey, nearly one-third of American adults complained of sleeplessness and nighttime pain.

> *In addition to its mechanical and psychological effects (such as anxiety and tension), pain may interact with neurotransmitters (chemicals responsible for transmitting nerve signals) in the brain.*

Another factor that affects sleep in chronic pain sufferers is depression. Many patients with chronic pain suffer from depression, which is an important cause of insomnia in general.

The treatment for sleep associated with pain should be directed primarily at alleviation of the pain along with short-term use of sleeping medications. This approach is preferred to prescribing sleeping medications on a long-term basis.

9. Why do we dream?

Dream is the "Royal Road to the Unconscious." So said Sigmund Freud in his seminal book, *The Interpretation of Dreams,* published in 1900. The Freudian theory postulated that repressed feelings are psychologically suppressed or hidden in the unconscious (unaware) mind and often manifested in dreams; sometimes these feelings are expressed as mental disorders or other psychologically determined physical ailments, according to this psychoanalytic theory. In Freud's view, most of the repressed feelings are determined by repressed sexual desires and may appear in dreams as symbols representing sexual organs.

In recent times, Freudian theory has fallen in disrepute. Today, modern scientists try to interpret dreams in anatomical and physiological terms. Nevertheless, we still cannot precisely define "what is dream" and "why we dream."

The field of dream research took a new turn in 1953, when two sleep scientists from the University of Chicago described the dream stage of sleep (or REM sleep) (see question #1). Approximately 80 percent of our dreams occur in REM sleep and 20 percent occur in NREM sleep. These two states alternate in a cyclical manner four to six times during our nighttime sleep. The last third of the night is dominated by REM sleep. Hence, we dream maximally during late night or in the early hours of the morning.

Approximately 80 percent of our dreams occur in REM sleep and 20 percent occur in NREM sleep.

Although we all dream, we may not always be able to recall these dreams. It is easier to recall REM dreams than NREM dreams. It is also easier to recall dreams if we are awakened immediately after the onset of REM dreams, rather than trying to remember them the next morning upon getting out of bed. REM dreams are often vivid, unrealistic, and bizarre. In contrast, dream recall, which sometimes may partially occur on awakening immediately from the NREM dream state, is more realistic. Most of our dreams take place in natural color, rather than black and white. In our dreams, we employ all five senses. In general, we use mostly our visual sensations, followed by auditory sensations; tactile, smell, and taste sensations are represented least.

Dreams can be pleasant, unpleasant, frightening, or sad. They generally reflect one's day-to-day activities. Fear, anxiety, and apprehension are incorporated into our dreams. In addition, stressful events of past or present may occupy our dreams. The dream scenes or events are rarely rational but often occur in an irrational manner with rapid change of scene, place, or people (or a bizarre mixture of these elements). Sometimes, lucid dreams may arise in which the dreamer seems to realize vividly that he or she is actually dreaming.

Some people have frequent, frightening dreams called nightmares or dream anxiety attacks, which appear to arise from intense, anxiety-provoking incidents in the dreamer's life. Nightmares are very common in children, beginning around the age of three to five years. They decrease in old age. Sometimes during fearful dreams, the individual may enact a past, stressful event (for example, a scene in a battlefield or a car accident).

The question of why we dream has both neurophysiological-neuroanatomical and psychological interpretations. Sleep scientists try to explain dreams in terms of the anatomical and physiological interpretations of REM (dream stage) sleep. During this stage, the synapses (contact points between nerve cells), nerve cells, and nerve fibers connecting various groups of nerve cells in the brain become activated. This activation begins in the brain stem (the deeper part in the base of the brain, which connects the main brain hemisphere with the spinal cord). The main brain hemisphere then synthesizes these signals and creates colorful or black-and-white images, giving rise to dreams. Similarly, signals sometimes become converted into auditory, tactile, or other sensations to create dream imagery. Why the nerve circuits are stimulated to cause dreaming is not clearly understood. We do know that REM sleep and NREM sleep alternate in a cyclical manner as a result of activation and inhibition of REM-on cells (those activated during REM sleep) and REM-off cells (those remaining quiet during REM sleep).

The main chemical agent causing activation of REM sleep is acetylcholine. Several other chemicals (for example, noradrenaline and serotonin) are responsible for inactivation of REM sleep. Thus an imbalance between these brain chemicals may cause nightmares, depression, and some other mental disorders.

Nobel laureate Francis Crick (who discovered the DNA structure) and Graham Mitchison have postulated that during dreams, we unburden the brain of useless information. Some have also suggested that memory consolidation takes place during dream stage of sleep. In addition, stories abound regarding artists, writers, and scientists who developed innovative ideas about their art, literature, and scientific projects during dreams.

10. Can certain medications cause excessive dreams?

Certain drugs can increase the dreams. For example, L-dopa, pergolide, and other drugs used to treat Parkinson's disease as well as beta blockers and related drugs used to treat high blood pressure can increase dreams and nightmares. Alcohol withdrawal may intensify dreams. In contrast, many antipsychotics and antidepressant medications as well as some sleeping medications (such as benzodiazepines) may suppress dreams. On withdrawal of these agents, an intensification of dreams and nightmares occurs.

Certain drugs can increase the dreams.

11. Do frequent dreams interfere with sleep?

Frequent, pleasant, or nonfrightening dreams generally do not interfere with sleep. Dreamers usually go back to sleep quickly. If the dreams occur daily or several times per week and awaken the dreamer, however, sleep may be disturbed because of exhaustion and failure to go back to sleep rapidly. Individuals who experience nightmares often wake up with sweating, fear, palpitation, and exhaustion. For this reason, frequent nightmares may interfere with sleep.

Frequent nightmares may interfere with sleep.

12. How common are sleep problems?

Day-to-day practice in medicine and various epidemiological surveys undertaken in the United States and elsewhere have made it abundantly clear that sleep problems are very common. Both insomnia and excessive sleepiness are prevalent in our society. In January 1993, a report of the National Commission of Sleep Disorders Research stated that millions of Americans are affected by sleep disorders, costing the society billions of dollars. Since the publication of that report, there has been a growing perception of sleep problems amongst the public and professions. Some statistics (see the Introduction) also attest to the seriousness of sleep problems in today's society. In reality, the problems are probably even more prevalent than revealed in the surveys, because no standardized definition of insomnia, sleep apnea, or excessive sleepiness exists.

Sleep deprivation is truly a curse of modern society.

A number of factors are associated with a greater prevalence of sleeplessness or insomnia: old age; female gender; lower socioeconomic status; being divorced, widowed, or separated; depression; stress; drug or alcohol abuse; and certain medical disorders. Sleep deprivation is truly a curse of modern society. In our competitive drive to move ahead in life, we often sacrifice our precious hours of sleep. As a result, we may suffer from excessive daytime sleepiness, which may actually cut our productivity and compromise our safety on the road. Many people do not realize that a sleep-deprived driver is as dangerous as a drunk driver.

Sleep apnea, a very serious condition, remains undiagnosed in thousands of people. Studies performed in Europe, the United States, and Israel clearly show that the prevalence rate for sleep apnea ranged from 1 percent to 4 percent. Only a handful of such patients are ever referred to a sleep specialist for diagnosis and treatment.

Sleep apnea (see question #20), a very serious condition, remains undiagnosed in thousands of people. Studies performed in Europe, the United States, and Israel clearly show that the prevalence rate for sleep apnea ranged from 1 percent to 4 percent. Only a handful of such patients are ever referred to a sleep specialist for diagnosis and treatment. Intensive education for both the medical profession and the public is needed to emphasize the existence and seriousness of a variety of disorders affecting our sleep. After all, sleep consumes one-third of our lives.

13. Are sleep disorders serious problems?

Sleep disorders are very serious problems. An occasional night of sleeplessness or daytime sleepiness once in a while is very common and does not need any special consideration. On the other hand, when sleep problems interfere with a person's quality of life and day-to-day function, he or she must consult a physician to avoid serious consequences. Sleep deprivation is pervasive in our society, and the ensuing sleepiness makes us prone to accidents in the workplace and on the road. Indeed, sleep deprivation has been cited as a major factor in many national and international catastrophes (see the Introduction).

Sleep deprivation is pervasive in our society, and the ensuing sleepiness makes us prone to accidents in the workplace and on the road. Indeed, sleep deprivation has been cited as a major factor in many national and international catastrophes.

14. What are common sleep problems?

Patients with sleep problems most commonly complain of the following:

- I cannot sleep.
- I cannot stay awake.
- I cannot sleep at the right time.
- I thrash and move about in bed, and I have repeated leg jerking.

These complaints address the entire field of sleep disturbances. "I cannot sleep" means that the person has trouble falling asleep or staying asleep and wakes up repeatedly throughout the night, including early hours of the morning. "I cannot stay awake" means that he or she falls asleep during the day at inappropriate places and under inappropriate circumstances. "I cannot sleep at the right time" means that the individual experiences difficulty going to sleep at the appropriate time; that is, he or she either goes to sleep late (for example, 3:00 A.M. to 5:00 A.M.) and wakes up late (for example, 11:00 A.M. to 1:00 P.M.), or goes to sleep early (for example, 8:00 P.M. to 9:00 P.M.) and wakes up early (for example, 3:00 A.M. to 5:00 A.M.). The last complaint—thrashing and leg jerking—refers to someone with periodic movements of the legs during sleep at night (witnessed by the bed partner) or thrashing, flailing, and other abnormal movements during sleep. These motions occur in a variety of sleep disorders.

> *Patients with sleep problems most commonly complain of the following: I cannot sleep; I cannot stay awake; I cannot sleep at the right time; I thrash and move about in bed, and I have repeated leg jerking.*

Sleep deprivation and insomnia are the two most common sleep problems in our society today. Other sleep problems include the following:

- Sleep apnea (cessation of breathing during sleep—see question #20)
- Restless legs syndrome (see question #38)
- Narcolepsy (see question #32)
- Sleep disturbances as a result of psychiatric, general medical, and neurological disorders
- Drug- and alcohol-related sleep problems

- Parasomnias (abnormal movements and behavior occurring during sleep)
- Circadian rhythm sleep disorders (mismatch of timing between the group of nerve cells functioning as a time clock in the center of the brain and the outside clock)

All of these problems are addressed briefly later in this book.

15. Is snoring a nuisance or a problem?

Before one can answer this question, it is important to know what causes snoring. Snoring is defined as a noisy (mild or loud) resonant breathing during sleep caused by the vibration of the soft tissues in the back of the throat behind the tongue. These soft tissues include the soft palate (a soft, muscular tissue in the back of the roof of the mouth), uvula (a soft, pear-shaped structure hanging below the soft palate behind the tongue), tonsils, back and side walls of the throat, and back of the tongue. Snoring is mainly caused by vibration of the uvula and the soft palate.

Snoring can be mild (occasional), moderate (frequent), and severe (very loud and frequent). During sleep, the muscle tone in the back of the throat, including that in the tongue and other muscles in the upper airway passage (through which air goes into the lungs), decreases; an especially marked decrement or absence of muscle tone occurs during the dream stage of sleep (REM sleep). This loss of muscle tone causes the tongue to go toward the back of the throat, slightly narrowing the upper airway and creating turbulence. The turbulence causes vibrations, mainly of the uvula and soft palate, which produce snoring. When a person is lying on his or her back, the tongue tends to go farther back; hence, snoring is worse in this position. In a severe case, snoring occurs in all body positions. Snoring becomes worse when muscle tone is greatly decreased (for example, when we are tired, drink alcohol, or take sleeping medication). In the presence of enlarged tonsils, a large and long uvula, or a bulky soft palate, the upper airway passage is narrowed even further, causing loud snoring. Partial obstruction in the nose (because of a cold or allergy that causes swelling of the tissues, for example, or a nasal septal deviation) may also contribute to snoring.

Snoring affects more men than women, and its prevalence increases with age. An important survey from San Marino, Italy, in the early 1980s found that 60 percent of men older than 60 years and 19 percent of the overall sample were habitual snorers. Later surveys confirmed the high prevalence of snoring in men. Those who smoke, lie on their back, are obese, and are physically inactive were found to be more likely to snore. Individuals with frequent loud snoring (habitual snorers) are more likely to doze off at the wheel and become involved in a traffic accident due to sleepiness and tiredness.

Mild snoring may be a social nuisance. In contrast, loud, frequent, almost nightly snoring may be the forerunner of a more serious disorder with severe long- and short-term consequences. That is, it may be the warning sign of something more sinister. Loud snoring may repeatedly disturb sleep for brief moments throughout the night. Although the snorer will not remember these brief interruptions in sleep, a recording of the electrical activities of the brain (EEG) will indicate recurrent periods of awakenings. Because the snorer does not get an adequate amount of sleep, he or she is sleep-deprived and prone to frequent sleepiness in the daytime. This condition is merely an intermediate stage between snoring and the next stage, when snoring becomes associated with periodic cessation of breathing throughout the night. This stage signifies a more serious condition than simple snoring—the snorer is now suffering from sleep apnea (see question #20).

Mild snoring may be a social nuisance. In contrast, loud, frequent, almost nightly snoring may be the forerunner of a more serious disorder with severe long- and short-term consequences.

16. My bed partner snores loudly, driving me crazy. He makes noises like a freight train. He also feels sleepy in the daytime. Should he use a snore guard or see a doctor?

If the snoring is loud enough (like the noise of a freight train) to drive the bed partner crazy, then certainly it is not just a nuisance. Additionally, if the snorer feels extremely sleepy in the daytime, then he or she is experiencing fragmented sleep (repeated brief awakenings at night), which causes daytime sleepiness. This condition may indicate that the individual is developing sleep apnea (see question #20).

If snoring occurs only when lying on the back, the person should try to sleep on his or her side. If the snoring and daytime sleepiness continue, then the individual should see a doctor for investigation of possible breathing disorders during sleep.

The best advice would be to see a physician, preferably a sleep specialist, who can make a positive diagnosis of breathing disorder during sleep early enough to prevent long-term adverse effects.

Numerous advertisements tout cures of snoring and sleep-related breathing problems. One should be wary of these antisnore devices, most of which do not benefit the sufferer or may reduce the intensity of snoring only temporarily. The best advice would be to see a physician, preferably a sleep specialist, who can make a positive diagnosis of breathing disorder during sleep early enough to prevent long-term adverse effects.

17. Is snoring related to any physical defect, and can snoring cause any physical illness or memory impairment?

The answer to question #15 discussed the causes of snoring. In addition to physical defects in the throat, other defects that may contribute to snoring include a receding chin, a large tongue, and a thick neck. Snoring by itself probably does not cause any physical illness or memory impairment. On the other hand, loud snoring for a long time secondarily may lead to mild swelling of the soft palate and uvula as a result of the repeated vibrations associated with snoring. This theory, however, remains controversial. Any memory impairment may actually be related to an associated sleep apnea, which causes blood oxygen levels to fall repeatedly during sleep at night, rather than to snoring itself.

In addition to physical defects in the throat, other defects that may contribute to snoring include a receding chin, a large tongue, and a thick neck.

18. Why does snoring become worse after I drink alcohol?

To understand the answer to this question, you must consider the mechanisms of snoring (see question #15). Snoring is associated with a reduction of muscle tone in the tongue and other muscles in the throat, which narrows the upper airway space. Alcohol has a direct depressant effect on these muscles, further reducing the muscle tone and allowing the tongue to move back farther, thereby narrowing the upper airway space. As a result of these alcohol-induced changes, the snoring worsens.

Alcohol has a direct depressant effect on these muscles, . . . allowing the tongue to move back farther, thereby narrowing the upper airway space. As a result of these alcohol-induced changes, the snoring worsens.

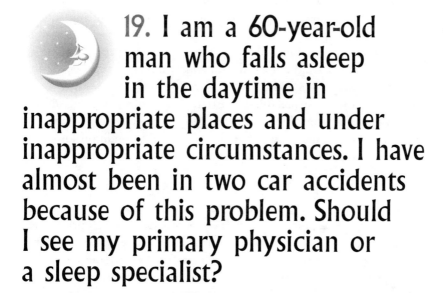

19. I am a 60-year-old man who falls asleep in the daytime in inappropriate places and under inappropriate circumstances. I have almost been in two car accidents because of this problem. Should I see my primary physician or a sleep specialist?

Symptoms of excessive sleepiness in the daytime, severe enough to nearly cause car accidents, suggest the presence of a serious condition that requires immediate attention. Many older men have such symptoms.

One common cause of such symptoms in an older man is sleep apnea

Symptoms of excessive sleepiness in the daytime, severe enough to nearly cause car accidents, suggest the presence of a serious condition that requires immediate attention. (see question #20). Many patients with this disorder remain undiagnosed. It is important to identify this condition early to prevent long-term adverse consequences. Fortunately, effective treatment is available for most patients suffering from this problem. To ensure that this condition is treated, you should see your primary care physician. He or she may suggest a consultation with a sleep specialist, who is in the best position to evaluate your condition by performing appropriate laboratory tests and suggesting optimal treatment.

20. What is sleep apnea?

The word "apnea" is derived from a Greek word meaning "for want of breath." Apnea—that is, cessation of breathing—occurring during sleep is called sleep apnea. Most people, especially after the age of 50 to 60, stop breathing momentarily a few times during nighttime sleep. This condition is normal and not a cause for concern. In a normal person, this breathing cessation may occur as many as five times per hour of sleep. To be significant, the breathing must stop at least ten seconds during sleep. Sometimes breathing may not stop completely but rather be reduced to half of the normal breathing volume, a condition known as hypopnea. Like sleep apnea, hypopnea has both short- and long-term adverse effects.

The medical profession has described three types of apneas—obstructive, central, and mixed types. The most common (and most serious) type is obstructive sleep apnea. In this type of abnormal breathing during sleep, the passage of inhaled air becomes obstructed in the region of the upper airway, most commonly at the level of the soft palate (see question #15). Consequently, air does not enter the lungs (the breathing organs responsible for maintaining normal respiration and blood oxygen at an optimal level), and the blood oxygen level tends to fall below the normal level. The diaphragm (the main muscle of breathing, separating the lower chest from the upper abdomen) and other chest wall muscles keep contracting, trying to overcome this obstruction in the upper airway. The brain then sends impulses, telling the subject to wake up. The person then wakes up with a loud snore. As soon as the individual wakes up, the muscle tone in the upper airway and the tongue returns to normal level. The tongue moves forward, the obstruction is relieved, and normal breathing resumes. This cycle repeats as soon as the individual returns to sleep.

In a mild case of obstructive sleep apnea, the cycle of apnea and normal breathing occurs only a few times. In severe cases, the cycle may repeat several hundred times, repeatedly reducing the blood oxygen level throughout the night and disturbing the individual's sleep. Because he or she obtains an inadequate amount of sleep, the person is sleep-deprived and sleeps excessively in the daytime in an inappropriate place and under inappropriate circumstances.

In central apnea, the airflow stops at the nose and mouth and the air does not enter the lungs. At the same time, the breathing effort by the diaphragm and other muscles of breathing stops. Central apnea is associated with a number of neurological disorders.

Mixed apnea is characterized by an initial period of central apnea, followed by a period of obstructive apnea. In the most common type of upper airway obstructive sleep apnea syndrome, the patient experiences many periods of mixed apneas as well as some central apneas.

Sleep apnea is more common in men than women, although its prevalence increases in postmenopausal women. The male hormone, testosterone, appears to predispose men to sleep apnea, whereas the female hormone, estrogen, acts as a deterrent to sleep apnea.

Researchers have not yet elucidated why the muscle tone in the upper airway falls excessively in patients with sleep apnea, producing an obstruction in the upper airway. In many patients, the uvula and soft palate are bulky and long, narrowing the airway passage. In children, large tonsils and adenoids (lymphoid tissues in the throat behind the nasal passage) narrow the air passage, causing loud snoring and sleep apnea. The nerve cells responsible for maintaining muscle tone in the tongue and other upper airway muscles appear to transmit fewer impulses to these tissues. To date, no evidence suggests that most patients with sleep apnea have a structural defect in the nerve cells of the brain stem (the lower part of the brain). Of course, neurological disorders (for example, stroke, tumor, trauma, multiple sclerosis) that affect the brain stem or brain may cause sleep apnea in many patients.

The most common (and most serious) type is obstructive sleep apnea. In this type of abnormal breathing during sleep, the passage of inhaled air becomes obstructed in the region of the upper airway, most commonly at the level of the soft palate.

Patients with sleep apnea present with a long history of loud snoring, stop breathing repeatedly during sleep at night (witnessed by a bed partner), and are plagued by recurrent awakenings. The major daytime symptom is excessive sleepiness at inappropriate times and under inappropriate circumstances, causing accidents and near-accidents during driving. In long-standing cases of severe sleep apnea, patients may be forgetful and men may have impotence. Although most patients are obese, the condition can also strike thin people. Sleep apnea's long-term serious consequences include hypertension, heart failure, irregular heart rhythm, stroke, myocardial infarction, and impairment of memory.

21. Can sleep apnea run in the family?

Sleep apnea may sometimes run in the family. In most patients, however, the condition is not familial. Risk factors (factors that may predispose a person to sleep apnea) include hypertension, obesity, alcoholism, and

Sleep apnea may sometimes run in the family.

minor abnormalities inside the mouth and face (long uvula, small upper airway space, receding chin). These risk factors may be inherited, which would explain the high occurrence of sleep apnea in some families. Adequate studies to determine familial incidence have not been undertaken.

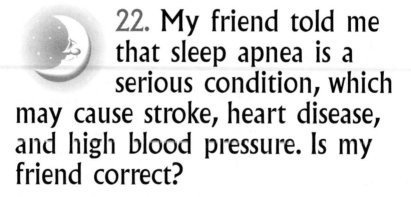

22. My friend told me that sleep apnea is a serious condition, which may cause stroke, heart disease, and high blood pressure. Is my friend correct?

Your friend is absolutely correct. There is an increased association between sleep apnea and stroke, heart disease (irregular heart rhythm and narrowing of the coronary arteries that supply blood to the heart), and high blood pressure. The question of whether sleep apnea by itself or obesity, high blood cholesterol, and alcoholism (all of which are risk factors for stroke, heart disease, high blood pressure, and sleep apnea) are actually responsible for an increased association of these diseases remains somewhat controversial. Most likely, sleep apnea is an important risk factor for all of these conditions. Approximately 50 percent of patients with sleep apnea have high blood pressure, whereas 30 percent of patients with high blood pressure have sleep apnea.

There is an increased association between sleep apnea and stroke, heart disease (irregular heart rhythm and narrowing of the coronary arteries that supply blood to the heart), and high blood pressure.

23. I have heard that people with sleep apnea may die suddenly in the middle of the night. Is this true?

Several reports have suggested that sudden death may occur in the middle and late part of the night, or in the early hours of the morning, in sleep apnea patients. This problem has been reported in patients who suffer from severe sleep apnea, which engenders repeated prolonged apneas, dangerously low blood oxygen levels, irregular heart rhythms, sleep disruption, and excessive daytime sleepiness. For this reason, it is important to see a physician when symptoms suggest sleep apnea to prevent long-term complications affecting the heart, brain, and circulatory system that could potentially elevate one's blood pressure and even cause sudden death.

It is important to see a physician when symptoms suggest sleep apnea to prevent long-term complications affecting the heart, brain, and circulatory system that could potentially elevate one's blood pressure and even cause sudden death.

24. My sleep specialist diagnosed sleep apnea for my daytime sleepiness and snoring, and suggested that I use a nasal mask, which will deliver air from the outside at a positive pressure to keep my upper airway passage open. What is this device supposed to do?

A nasal mask delivers continuous positive airway pressure (CPAP) through the nose. It consists of a small, portable machine weighing roughly 10 to 15 lb, which can sit on a lamp table by the side of the bed. The CPAP device comprises the following components: a face mask, head straps, a tube or hose connecting a pressure generator or a blower, and a valve to adjust the pressure of the air delivered through the nose into the back of the throat.

With this device, the air from outside, which is delivered at a positive pressure, separates the back of the throat from the uvula, soft palate, and tongue. The column of air acts as a pneumatic splint to keep the airway passage open during sleep. As a consequence, despite the excessive reduction of muscle tone in the throat and the tongue, outside air continues to flow into the lungs. The patient breathes normally, oxygen levels in the blood do not fall, and snoring is eliminated because no turbulence results from narrowing of the air passage. The patient sleeps soundly, without any apnea-related repeated interruptions. He or she does not feel excessively sleepy in the daytime and, as a result, feels energetic and active and does not complain of fatigue, lack of concentration, forgetfulness, or impotence.

Patients must wear the nasal mask device every night during sleep; otherwise, the symptoms will recur.

Patients must wear the nasal mask device every night during sleep; otherwise, the symptoms will recur. Hence, CPAP treatment is not a cure but rather gives symptomatic relief. The device may be uncomfortable in the beginning, but approximately 75 percent of patients become used to it in the course of two to three weeks. Some individuals may complain of difficulty breathing when the same pressure is delivered during both inhalation and expiration (exhaling the air). For such patients, the CPAP device can be adjusted so that it delivers high-pressure air during inspiration and lower-pressure air during expiration, causing bilevel delivery of positive airway pressure.

25. What are some problems associated with the use of a mask delivering positive airway pressure continuously?

The patient may encounter several problems with CPAP, but most can be corrected. Some patients become very uncomfortable—even claustrophobic—when using the nasal mask. In most cases, explanation and assurance suffice to relieve their anxiety. If the mask is not tightly fitted, the air may leak around the edges, irritating the skin of the face and the eyes. Some people complain of dryness and stuffiness of the nose, which can be improved by attaching a humidifier (delivering warm or cold moist air) to the CPAP machine. If the mask is too tight, it may cause chafing of the bridge of the nose. The solution is to loosen the head gear slightly and use a soft pad over the bridge of the nose. If these measures fail, then a different type of mask may be used with benefit.

The patient may encounter several problems with CPAP, but most can be corrected.

Some people complain of dryness of the mouth because of mouth breathing; in these cases, a chin strap to keep the mouth shut will help. Some patients—particularly those suffering from nasal allergy—may complain of nasal congestion and a runny nose. In these patients, nasal decongestant drops may prove helpful.

Other problems may include psychological worries about the patient's relationship with his or her bed partner and a feeling of invalidity. The bed partner may also be psychologically disturbed by the prospect of sleeping with a person who is wearing a mask and head gear, resembling a man or woman from outer space. A thoughtful discussion with both bed partners will allay such psychological fears.

26. I am a 40-year-old single woman. I can fall asleep easily but wake up between 3:00 and 4:00 A.M. and cannot get back to sleep again. What should I do?

Early morning awakening is a very common sleep-related problem. Before anything can be done about it, it is important to try to find out why the patient wakes up late at night or in the early hours of the morning. This type of sleeplessness is a symptom, rather than a disease.

A common cause for such a problem is depression. The individual and his or her physician must find out whether symptoms of depression are present. Do you feel sad? Do you feel lonely? Do you feel like sitting and doing nothing? Do you suffer from a lack of energy? Do you feel exhausted and tired all the time? Did something happen at home or in the workplace, which may have made you feel depressed?

Early morning awakening is a very common sleep-related problem. . . . This type of sleeplessness is a symptom, rather than a disease.

Another cause of early morning awakening is drinking alcohol at bedtime. Many people drink alcohol to get to sleep. Alcohol acts as a depressant to the central nervous system. When the blood alcohol level falls, however, rebound awakening occurs; it causes you to wake up early in the morning.

Other causes of early morning awakening may include intense fearful dreams or nightmares, waning of the effects of a sleeping medication taken earlier in the evening, and dependence on sleeping medications. If you cannot explain your problem or think you may suffer from depression, consult a physician. Such problems are treatable and you may not actually suffer from sleeplessness.

27. I toss and turn in bed and it takes me two to three hours to go to sleep. In the daytime, I feel irritable and tired. What is happening to me?

In this case, the culprit is sleep-onset insomnia. An estimated one-third of the population suffers from some form of insomnia (either sleep-onset or sleep maintenance insomnia with repeated awakenings). In 10 percent of all people, this condition is a persistent problem. If you do not receive adequate hours of sleep, you will feel irritable and tired the next day. Occasional difficulty in falling asleep is very common and is of no consequence. For persistent problems, however, you should seek professional help. In such cases, the complaint may be related to various types of temporary and long-standing sleeplessness (see question #28).

An estimated one-third of the population suffers from some form of insomnia (either sleep-onset or sleep maintenance insomnia with repeated awakenings). In 10 percent of all people, this condition is a persistent problem.

28. What causes temporary and long-standing sleeplessness?

Sleeplessness or insomnia may be due to many causes. Sometimes, a given individual may experience more than one cause. Also, different causes may produce different types of insomnia (such as sleep-onset or sleep maintenance insomnia). For example, anxiety may cause sleep-onset problems, whereas depression may lead to early morning insomnia.

Transient and short-term insomnia refers to insomnia lasting as long as three weeks; sleeplessness lasting for more than three weeks constitutes chronic insomnia. The most common cause of transient insomnia is a change in the sleeping environment—for example, sleeping in an unfamiliar environment such as a hotel room, sleep laboratory, or a nursing home or hospital. Unpleasant room temperature, humidity, or excessive environmental noise may also lead to transient insomnia. Acute medical or surgical illnesses and stressful life events (for example, divorce, stress at work, loss of employment, death of a loved one, preparing for an examination the next day) might also cause transient and short-term insomnia. Some medications (see question #86) or eating a heavy meal in the evening may cause short-term insomnia. Likewise, taking an airplane flight that crosses several time zones (see question #75) may cause transient insomnia. Many of the almost 5 million shift workers in the United States are also prone to short-term or chronic insomnia in addition to other physical problems.

The most common cause of transient insomnia is a change in the sleeping environment—for example, sleeping in an unfamiliar environment such as a hotel room, sleep laboratory, or a nursing home or hospital.

Chronic insomnia may result from a variety of psychiatric, medical, or neurological illnesses or primary sleep disorders (such as restless legs syndrome, poor sleep hygiene, circadian rhythm sleep disorders, insomnia of unknown cause, or insomnia related to some psychological factors). Other causes of chronic insomnia include chronic drug and alcohol use. Some sleep specialists think that psychological and psychiatric disorders are the most common causes of such long-standing sleep problems. Many people with insomnia, however, do not have psychiatric or psychological problems.

Chronic insomnia may result from a variety of psychiatric, medical, or neurological illnesses or primary sleep disorders (such as restless legs syndrome, poor sleep hygiene, circadian rhythm sleep disorders, insomnia of unknown cause, or insomnia related to some psychological factors).

29. Can sleeplessness interfere with memory, intellect, and creativity?

Every individual has a certain minimum requirement for sleep (see question #3). If this minimum sleep requirement is not met, symptoms of insomnia will interfere with the person's life and efficiency at work. These symptoms may include irritability, lack of con-

Sleep deprivation experiments have clearly shown that these problems are temporary rather than a permanent impairment.

centration, tiredness, sleepiness in the daytime, and temporary forgetful-ness. Although they may interfere with creativity and judgment, such symp-toms are unlikely to interfere with long-term memory and intellect. Sleep deprivation experiments have clearly shown that these problems are tem-porary rather than a permanent impairment (see questions #4 and #5).

30. What can I do for my sleeplessness?

If your problem is more than just an occasional occurrence and interferes with the quality of your life at home and work, you must seek help. First, you may try some common-sense measures to improve your sleep (see question #80). If the problem persists, you must consult a physician (preferably a sleep specialist), who is in the best position to determine the cause of your sleeplessness after obtaining a detailed history and per-forming a physical examination. In most cases, the findings will be that insomnia is not a disease but rather a symptom.

The specialist will advise you about appropriate treatment, which could consist of sleeping medications or nondrug treatment, or a combi-nation of the two measures. Sleeping medications are generally prescribed for transient and short-term insomnia. In contrast, non-drug treatment, with or without intermittent use of sleeping medications, is the mainstay of treatment for chronic insomnia.

Nonpharmacologic or nondrug treatment includes sleep hygiene measures (see question #80), relaxation therapy and biofeedback, stimulus control therapy, sleep restric-tion, and patient education about sleep habits, atti-tudes toward sleep, and cognitive-behavioral therapy. Relaxation therapy incorporates progressive muscle relaxation and biofeedback to reduce the arous-ing stimuli. Stimulus control therapy is directed at discouraging the learned association between the bedroom and wakefulness, and reestablishing the bedroom as the major stimulus for sleep. As part of this therapy, patients are advised to do the following:

Sleeping medications are generally prescribed for transient and short-term insomnia. In contrast, non-drug treatment, with or without intermittent use of sleeping medications, is the mainstay of treatment for chronic insomnia.

- Go to bed when you are sleepy.
- Do not watch television, eat, or worry while in bed.

- Use the bed only for sleep and intimacy.
- If you are unable to fall asleep within 20 minutes, get out of bed, go to another room, do something relaxing (such as listening to music or reading light books), and then go back to bed when sleepy.
- Wake up at a fixed time each morning.
- Do not take a nap.

31. Can sleeplessness lead to psychological or psychiatric problems, cause someone to develop a psychopathic personality, or even lead a person to commit murder and practice other violent behaviors?

A close interrelationship exists between chronic insomnia and psychiatric problems. In several surveys and studies, researchers have found that insomnia commonly coexists or precedes the onset of a number of psychiatric illnesses. The psychiatric conditions most commonly associated with insomnia include depression and anxiety. Major psychiatric illness, such as schizophrenia, may cause insomnia or hypersomnia as well. Individuals with insomnia are much more likely to develop a new psychiatric disorder, particularly major depression within 6 to 12 months of the onset of their sleeplessness. It should also be remembered that individuals with insomnia often complain of anxiety and depression.

> *A close interrelationship exists between chronic insomnia and psychiatric problems. In several surveys and studies, researchers have found that insomnia commonly coexists or precedes the onset of a number of psychiatric illnesses.*

Most insomniacs do not develop a psychopathic personality. Conversely, a person with a psychopathic personality may suffer from sleeplessness. Insomnia does not lead to homicidal or violent behaviors unlike some other sleep problems, such as sleep walking (see question #72).

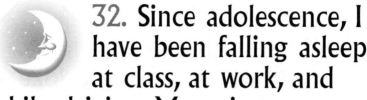

32. Since adolescence, I have been falling asleep at class, at work, and while driving. My primary care physician told me I may have narcolepsy. What is narcolepsy?

The French physician Gelineau first coined the term "narcolepsy," which is derived from two Greek words: *narcos* (meaning "sleep") and *lepsis* (meaning "sudden occurrence like a seizure"). Narcolepsy is characterized by an irresistible and uncontrollable desire to fall asleep. The most common age of onset is between 15 and 20 years. The prevalence of narcolepsy is estimated at 3 to 6 persons per 10,000 population.

In this disorder, the patient falls asleep in inappropriate places and under inappropriate circumstances. For example, he or she may fall asleep while driving, talking, eating, playing, working, listening to lectures, watching movies or television, being in boring or monotonous circumstances, and even during sexual intercourse. The spells are generally brief, lasting from a few minutes to 15 to 30 minutes. Upon awakening, the narcoleptic individual generally feels refreshed. The attacks persist throughout the patient's lifetime, although treatment provides relief to most people. The diagnosis of this condition is often delayed, however, because many patients are labeled as lazy and inattentive or thought to have misused drugs and alcohol.

Narcolepsy is characterized by an irresistible and uncontrollable desire to fall asleep. The most common age of onset is between 15 and 20 years.

All patients with narcolepsy have sleep attacks and excessive daytime sleepiness. Many also exhibit other symptoms. Approximately 70 percent of narcoleptics have cataplexy (see question #33). Other symptoms that are present in almost half of all such patients include sleep paralysis (a feeling that one cannot move the whole body, one side of the body, or one arm or leg at the onset of sleep or when just waking up), vivid hallucinatory and fearful dreams, and nighttime sleep disturbance.

33. I suffer from irresistible sleep attacks. Also, on hearing a joke, I tend to go limp momentarily without loss of consciousness. My doctor told me I may have cataplexy. What is cataplexy?

Cataplexy is a momentary loss of muscle tone without loss of conscious-ness, causing a person to fall to the ground; some-times, just the head may fall forward due to the loss of neck muscle tone. These episodes generally occur following emotional excitement (for example, hearing a joke or becoming angry). This symptom makes the diagnosis of narcolepsy almost certain, but is not present in all patients with narcolepsy. In some narcolepsy patients, the description of the catapletic episodes is questionable. Generally, sleep attacks and sleepiness occur early during the course of disease, and cataplexy occurs later during narcolepsy—perhaps even months or years later.

Cataplexy is a momentary loss of muscle tone without loss of consciousness, causing a person to fall to the ground; sometimes, just the head may fall forward due to the loss of neck muscle tone.

34. Can narcolepsy run in the family?

Narcolepsy can run in the family. Studies have shown that 1 to 2 percent of first-degree relatives of nar-coleptic patients present with symptoms of nar-colepsy, compared with 0.02 to 0.18 percent of the general population. Twin studies, however, have shown that this genetic influence is not very strong. Additional environmental factors are important in the causation of narcolepsy.

Narcolepsy can run in the family. Studies have shown that 1 to 2 percent of first-degree relatives of narcoleptic patients present with symptoms of narcolepsy.

35. How is narcolepsy diagnosed?

Most important for the diagnosis of narcolepsy is a consultation with a physician who spends time taking a detailed history of the illness and then performing a physical examination. First, the physician evaluates the nature of the patient's symptoms of sleep attacks and daytime sleepiness. After taking a thorough history, the doctor will perform a physical examination to determine whether any physical illnesses may have caused excessive sleepiness. When the physician suspects narcolepsy, he or she orders laboratory tests to confirm the diagnosis before treating the patient.

Most important for the diagnosis of narcolepsy is a consultation with a physician who spends time taking a detailed history of the illness and then performing a physical examination.

The two most important laboratory tests for confirmation of diagnosis of narcolepsy are an overnight sleep study (see question #43) followed by a multiple sleep latency test (see question #44). In the overnight sleep study, the narcoleptic patient may fall asleep very quickly and his or her dream stage of sleep (REM sleep—see question #1) may occur earlier than normal. Multiple sleep latency tests, which consist of four to five nap studies, will show that the narcoleptic goes to sleep much faster than normal people and enters REM sleep in two or more nap studies. Taking into consideration the patient's symptoms, these laboratory abnormalities confirm the clinical suspicion of narcolepsy.

The two most important laboratory tests for confirmation of diagnosis of narcolepsy are an overnight sleep study followed by a multiple sleep latency test.

36. How is narcolepsy treated?

The treatment of narcolepsy includes both drug and nondrug therapies. The physician may prescribe central nervous system stimulants for sleep attacks and sleepiness, carefully monitoring the dose, the progress of the illness, and any side effects of the medication. The most commonly used drugs are Ritalin, amphetamines, and a new drug called Modafinil

(Provigil). Because of their potential for abuse, use of such medications must be closely monitored by the physician. Drug therapies for cataplexy, sleep paralysis, and vivid hallucinatory dreams include antidepressant agents.

Nondrug treatments for narcolepsy involve following general sleep hygiene measures, which are common-sense measures (see question #80) intended to regularize the sleep schedule, as well as short daytime naps. Scheduling short sleep periods (lasting 20 to 30 minutes) during the daytime may help prevent sleep attacks and sleepiness temporarily. Joining a narcolepsy support group (see question #100) may aid the patient in understanding the disease and coping with his or her problem.

The treatment of narcolepsy includes both drug and nondrug therapies.

37. I am a 65-year-old man. I have terrible feelings in my legs when I am in bed preparing to go to sleep. I must keep moving my legs or get out of bed and walk around to get relief. This condition is driving me crazy and preventing me from getting to sleep. Some doctors told me that it is psychological. Is that true?

The symptoms described here strongly suggest that the patient may have restless legs syndrome (RLS; see question #38). Karl Ekbom, a Swedish physician, first named and gave a comprehensive description of this disease in 1944–1945. A search of the literature revealed that similar symptoms were described in patients more than 300 years ago by an English physician, Thomas Willis, although he did not name this disease.

Many misconceptions persist about RLS. Because of a lack of knowledge on the part of many physicians and the public, it remains an undiagnosed or underdiagnosed condition. The symptoms are often thought to be psychological in origin because of their unusual nature. Because of their tendency to occur in the evening or night, physicians do not find any abnormality on physical examination. Restlessness may sometimes be a manifestation of a psychiatric or psychological condition, but this symptom is quite different from the clinical features of a patient suffering from RLS (see question #38).

RLS remains an undiagnosed or underdiagnosed condition.

To receive a definitive diagnosis, a patient with the symptoms described in the question should see a physician with a special interest in sleep disorders, especially in RLS. The office of the Restless Legs Syndrome Foundation (see question #100) can direct you to a physician in your area. Several medications can bring relief from RLS's symptoms, so it is important to sort things out.

A few years ago, a group of physicians (including the author of this book) who had a special interest in RLS began an effort to develop some minimal clinical criteria for making a diagnosis of RLS. Currently, no single laboratory test can definitively confirm this diagnosis. Likewise, no blood test, nerve test, brain wave test, or X-ray examination of the brain (including the MRI) is capable of proving the presence of this condition. Because no good epidemiological studies exist for RLS and because a standard is needed for research purposes, the International RLS study group published four minimal criteria for the diagnosis of RLS:

- A desire to move the limbs, usually associated with intense, disagreeable, and uncomfortable feelings, at least partly and temporarily relieved by activities

- Motor restlessness, mostly in the legs but also occasionally in the arms

- Worsening of symptoms or their exclusive presence while lying or sitting

- Worsening of symptoms in the evening or night.

Individuals suffering from RLS develop an intense, disagreeable feeling, variously described as creeping, crawling, tingling, burning, aching, cramping, vise-like, itchy, much like bugs crawling under the skin, and rarely painful. These uncomfortable sensations occur mostly between the knees and ankles, causing an intense urge to move the legs to relieve these feelings. They also prevent the patient from going to sleep. Indeed, sometimes the individual will wake up in the middle of the night with these feelings, which prevents him or her from having a good-quality sleep.

Many patients try all types of tricks to obtain relief from their condition. They move, massage, or rub their legs; they get out of bed to walk around. These maneuvers may temporarily relieve the symptoms. For some individuals, a hot bath may prove helpful. In more severe cases, symptoms may even occur in the daytime when the patients are sitting or lying down. Long travel in a car, train, or plane may be particularly distressing. Many individuals with RLS find it impossible to sit for any length of time in a movie house or theater; they find that they must stand in the back of the theater to relieve the intense, disagreeable feelings in their legs.

Other criteria developed by the International RLS study group to define RLS include sleep disturbance, abnormal movements of the legs, and familial occurrence. Most patients with this condition consult a physician when they reach middle age or their later years. On questioning, however, most will report having the symptoms since a young age; because the symptoms were milder then, patients often did not bother to see a physician when they first arose. A few cases of RLS have been described in children, and an association between childhood RLS and attention deficit hyperactivity disorder has been reported.

The course of RLS is generally chronic, but sometimes remission occurs. The condition may be first noted during pregnancy; it can also be exacerbated by pregnancy. Likewise, ingestion of caffeinated beverages may make the symptoms worse.

38. My husband tells me that I keep moving my legs during sleep. In the daytime, I feel tired and irritable. I do not seem to have quality sleep at night. Do I have RLS?

The symptoms described here suggest that the patient may have periodic limb movements in sleep (PLMS). In PLMS, certain kinds of movements affect mostly the legs but occasionally the arms; these movements occur in a periodic or semiperiodic manner during sleep, mostly during NREM sleep (see question #1). The patient moves his or her legs in a periodic fashion, for perhaps an hour or so, and then stops moving. The movements recur intermittently throughout the night. During the dream stage of sleep (REM sleep), they generally stop. The bed partner may be able to describe your movements, which usually include bending of the toes and foot upward, sometimes bending of the knees, and occasionally bending of the arms and forearms every 20 to 40 seconds (range of 5 to 90 seconds).

During some of these movements, the patient may briefly wake up. Although the PLMS patient may be unaware of this awakening, a sleep specialist can detect it by looking at the brain waves (EEG) during an overnight polysomnographic study (see question #43). The brain wakes up briefly (3 to 14 seconds), causing the EEG to show a change from sleep to waking rhythms (see question #1). If you briefly wake up in this manner repeatedly throughout the night, your sleep will not be consolidated. The resulting poor quality of sleep will lead to daytime fatigue and sleepiness. Whether PLMS causes sleep disturbance, giving rise to daytime fatigue and tiredness, remains somewhat controversial.

At least 80 percent of patients with RLS have PLMS. In addition, PLMS may occur as an isolated condition or be associated with a variety of other medical and neurological illnesses, medications, or primary sleep disorders.

At least 80 percent of patients with RLS have PLMS. In addition, PLMS may occur as an isolated condition or be associated with a variety of other medical and neurological illnesses, medications, or primary sleep disorders. In particular, some antidepressant medications may aggravate these movements. Sometimes PLMS may occur in normal individuals, particularly elderly subjects.

To ascertain whether the patient has RLS, the physician will first ask several questions to decide whether he or she meets the minimal criteria established by the International RLS study group and then perform a thorough physical examination.

39. Does RLS run in the family?

RLS may sometimes be hereditary. In approximately 30 percent of all cases, a close relative may exhibit similar symptoms, which suggests that

RLS may sometimes be hereditary. In approximately 30 percent of all cases, a close relative may exhibit similar symptoms, which suggests that RLS follows a dominant mode of inheritance.

RLS follows a dominant mode of inheritance. First- and second-degree relatives of RLS patients are affected more often than controls are. This risk is particularly apparent in patients with an early age of onset. As yet, no large-scale, population-based study has precisely determined the risk of RLS occurring in close relatives.

40. What is the cause of RLS?

Researchers have been trying to identify the cause of RLS since its description more than half a century ago. Today, we know a great deal about RLS—but not exactly what causes RLS or which part of the nervous system, if any, is affected in RLS patients. Is the problem located in the brain, brain stem (the lower part of the brain, which is connected to main portion of brain and controls vital function such as circulation, respiration, and sleep), or the spinal cord (the long, tubular structure of the central nervous system that connects to the brain stem and runs through the vertebral column)?

Based on research studies, it appears that the problem lies somewhere between the main portion of the brain (the cerebral hemisphere) and the spinal cord. Response-to-treatment and other studies point to a problem with a chemical called dopamine, which is deficient in Parkinson's disease.

Based on research studies, it appears that the problem lies somewhere between the main portion of the brain (the cerebral hemisphere) and the spinal cord. Response-to-treatment and other studies point to a problem with a chemical called dopamine, which is deficient in Parkinson's disease. However, the problem with dopamine in patients with RLS seems to involve a different mechanism than is present in Parkinson's disease. Neurophysiologic and MRI studies suggest that a dysfunction may occur somewhere in the region of the brain stem. In most cases of RLS, no clear cause is found.

In some patients, RLS symptoms may arise secondary to other disorders, such as an abnormality of the nerves conducting impulses outside the central nervous system, chronic failure of the kidneys (the organs responsible for urine production and excretion from the body), iron deficiency, diabetes mellitus, or chronic joint disease. RLS may also be associated with or caused by some medication (for example, antidepressants). Because we do not know RLS's exact cause, we can only treat the symptoms but not cure the disease at present. The good news is that most patients get relief, although they may have to continue taking medication indefinitely.

41. How does a sleep specialist diagnose a sleep problem?

A sleep specialist evaluates a sleep problem by first taking a history and then performing a physical examination. Laboratory tests may then be ordered, if necessary.

Initially, the physician obtains information regarding the patient's sleep complaints. This history should include not only the problems at sleep onset or during sleep at night, but also symptoms occurring during the daytime. Many patients will complain of difficulty falling asleep, staying asleep, or waking up early in the morning. They may also have excessive sleepiness, irritability, or fatigue during the daytime. Therefore, it is important to have information regarding symptoms during the entire 24-hour period. In addition, the history should cover sleep habits (for example, bed time, waking time, number of awakenings during sleep at night) and information about drug and alcohol consumption; psychiatric, medical, surgical, and neurological illnesses; history of previous illnesses; and family history. The family history is important because some sleep disorders run in the family, including narcolepsy, RLS, sleep apnea, and sleep walking.

A sleep specialist evaluates a sleep problem by first taking a history and then performing a physical examination.

It is also important to interview the patient's bed partner or care giver or, in case of children, the parent to evaluate whether the patient has any abnormal movements, behavior, breathing patterns, or snoring during sleep. The physician should inquire about stress at home, work, or school, as it may cause sleep disturbance.

Sometimes, the sleep specialist will ask the patient to fill out a sleep questionnaire containing a list of questions relating to sleep complaints or ask the patient to maintain a sleep log or diary. This log, which is kept over two weeks, will document bed time, arousing time, amount of time needed to fall asleep, nighttime awakenings, total sleep time, mood on arousal and during the daytime, and any daytime naps.

The physical examination is important to uncover any general medical or neurological illnesses, which may cause sleep disorders or be risk factors for sleep dysfunction. After taking a thorough history and completing the physical examination, the sleep specialist will be in a position to suspect the nature of the patient's sleep problem and can order appropriate laboratory tests, if necessary, to confirm the suspected diagnosis. Following confirmation of the diagnosis, the physician will be able to design an appropriate treatment for the problem.

42. What are some important laboratory tests for evaluating sleep problems?

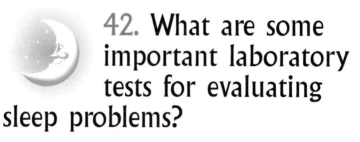

Laboratory tests need to be performed to diagnose some sleep problems. For example, in patients complaining of excessive sleepiness in the daytime, those having difficulty in sleeping at the right time, and those experiencing abnormal movements and behavior frequently during nighttime sleep, laboratory tests are essential to make a definite diagnosis. Such studies are generally not needed in patients with uncomplicated insomnia, but they are necessary if insomnia is associated with periodic limb movements in sleep (see question #38) or if the patient is suspected of having sleep apnea. Of course, laboratory tests are needed to diagnose the primary condition if the sleep problem is thought to result from a general medical or neurological disorder.

The two most important laboratory tests are overnight polysomnographic study and multiple daytime sleep study.

The two most important laboratory tests are overnight polysomnographic study (see question #43) and multiple daytime sleep study (see question #44). Other tests, which may be needed in special situations, include actigraphy, video-polysomnographic study, and prolonged monitoring of brain wave tests (EEG).

Actigraphy involves wearing a watch-like device on the wrist or ankle to monitor activities of the body resulting from body movements—the actigraph is a motion detector. Presumably, we lie relatively immobile during sleep, so the device should register few movements, whereas during wakefulness the actigraph records excessive body movements. In this way, actigraph indirectly estimates the amount of sleep and wakefulness as well as the time of sleep onset and offset. The recording is important in patients with circadian rhythm sleep disorders (see questions #7 and #77), which cause them to experience difficulty in getting to sleep at the right time.

Video-polysomnographic study obtains continuous video monitoring during sleep at night and measures many physiological characteristics (see question #43) during an overnight study. This test is important to observe any abnormal movements and behavior that may occur during sleep at night so as to make a correct diagnosis. It can differentiate seizures or convulsive movements from other types of abnormal movements and behavior occurring during nighttime sleep. It is important to make a correct diagnosis of each type of movement and behavior in different conditions.

In suspected cases of seizure disorder or epilepsy occurring predominantly at night, it is very important to obtain a prolonged EEG (recording of electrical activity of the brain) both during the daytime and nighttime. In addition, other physiological characteristics during nighttime sleep should be recorded (see question #43).

43. What is an overnight sleep study? Is it uncomfortable?

An overnight sleep study is a recording of activities from many body systems and organs (physiological characteristics) during sleep at night. It is a painless procedure that should not cause any discomfort to the patient. No needles are used, and the subject will not receive any electrical shock. The person having the test is connected by many sensors and wires to the equipment that records the various activities. A typical recording registers the electrical activities of the brain (EEG), the muscles (electromyogram, or EMG), eye movements (electro-oculogram, or EOG), heart rhythm (electrocardiogram), respiratory pattern, snoring, body position, and blood oxygen saturation continuously during sleep at night.

Electrical activities of the brain or the electroencephalogram are recorded by using two to ten channels of a polygraph. The polygraph is somewhat similar to the "lie detector" machine (polygraph test) used in some court cases. Of course, an overnight study takes place in the sleep laboratory, and it records many more physiological characteristics than those studied during lie detector tests.

For EEG recording, electrodes or sensors (small, cup-shaped or flat disks measuring about 5 to 6 mm) are attached with glue to the scalp; these attachments are painless. The sensors are connected by wires to the amplifiers of the polygraph. The electrical activities generated on the surface of the brain are tiny currents that must be augmented or amplified before they can be recognized on the monitor of the computer or recording paper; hence, an amplifier is an essential part of the polygraph. Most laboratories now use computers for recording rather than voluminous amounts of recording paper throughout the night.

To record eye movements (EOG), surface disks are placed over the upper corner of one eye and the lower corner of the other eye. Electrical activities of the muscles (EMG) are routinely recorded by placing sensors over the chin and outer aspects of the upper legs below the knees bilaterally. EEG, EOG, and EMG readings are used to identify the different sleep stages.

In most cases, the respiration pattern is recorded by using three channels. A sensor is placed over the upper lip below the nose to record airflow

An overnight sleep study is a recording of activities from many body systems and organs (physiological characteristics) during sleep at night.

through the nose and mouth. A band across the chest and another band across the abdomen (strain gauges) register respiratory effort by recording chest and abdominal excursion during breathing. In the most common type of sleep apnea, the airflow channels recording the activities from the sensors placed below the nose show no activity or markedly reduced activity, whereas the channels registering chest and abdominal movements are deflected in opposite directions, indicating obstruction in the upper airway passage in the back of the tongue.

Blood oxygen saturation is recorded throughout the night by using a finger clip. The finger clip registers changes in the color of hemoglobin (blood pigment); the color, which is shown on a monitor by a number (for example, 90 to 100 percent in a normal person), indicates blood oxygen saturation (oxygen is carried in the hemoglobin of the blood). In patients with sleep apnea, the oxygen saturation of the blood falls below 90 percent when the breathing (airflow) stops.

To record snoring, a small microphone is attached over the front of the neck. Body position during sleep is monitored through a position sensor over the shoulder. The degree of sleep apnea is worse when a person lies on his or her back. In a routine overnight recording, one channel is used to record electrical signals of the heartbeat (electrocardiogram) via sensors or the electrodes placed over the upper chest.

After placement of all sensors, the connecting wires are gathered into a bundle and attached to the board next to the patient. This board is then connected by wires going through the walls or the ceiling of the bedroom to the main polygraphic machine or computer to an adjacent room, where the technician will monitor a paperless recording (or the paper in the machine, if such a recording is used), and make necessary adjustments to obtain the optimal recording. If any of the electrodes (sensors and detectors) are moved, creating artifacts in the recording, the technician will enter the patient's room and reposition the sensor so that artifacts are eliminated. The technician will also watch the video if such a recording is used (most laboratories generally use simultaneous video recording to observe any abnormal movements and behavior during sleep).

The patient generally comes to the laboratory in the evening around 9:00 P.M. The technician explains the procedure to the patient and tries to set the patient at ease. Making the connections and preparations of the machine generally takes about an hour. The technician then turns the lights off at the approximate bedtime of the particular individual and asks the person to get ready to sleep. If the patient must get up in the middle of the night to visit the bathroom, the bundle of wires can be easily disconnected from the machine and clipped to the patient's pajamas or nightwear, then reconnected again on returning to bed. In the morning, the technician will come to the room around 6:00 to 7:00 A.M. to turn the lights on, remove the electrodes from the patient's skin, and clean the skin surface. The patient is then ready to go home unless he or she is scheduled to have a multiple daytime sleep study (see question #44).

44. What is a multiple daytime sleep study?

A multiple daytime sleep study, also known as a multiple sleep latency test (MSLT), is a very important test to assess the severity of daytime sleepiness. MSLT is an absolute necessity for the diagnosis of narcolepsy (see question #35) but is also important to assess the overall severity of sleep apnea and other conditions associated with excessive daytime sleepiness. This test is performed the day after completion of an overnight sleep study.

To correctly interpret the significance of the findings in the MSLT, the sleep pattern (total number of hours of sleep and number of awakenings) and the quality of sleep the night before the test must be known. Any impaired and fragmented sleep during the previous night may cause short sleep latency and sleep onset rapid eye movements, thereby introducing confounding factors to the diagnosis of narcolepsy and other disorders causing excessive daytime sleepiness.

MSLT is performed every two hours for four to five recordings, and each recording lasts as long as 20 minutes. The test is conducted two to three hours after the final wake-up in the morning following the all-night study. For example, the test can be performed at 9:00 A.M., 11:00 A.M., 1:00 P.M., and 3:00 P.M. The electrical activities of the brain (EEG), chin muscles (EMG), and eye movements (EOG) are recorded during the 20-minute test. The electrodes for these recordings would have been in place from the overnight study. Patients are asked to refrain from drinking coffee and smoking in the morning. Following breakfast and explanation of the test, the technician turns the lights off and asks the patient to lie down and try to go to sleep. In between the tests, the patient must stay awake and read, walk around, or watch television but must not fall asleep; otherwise, the significance of the findings will remain questionable.

The sleep specialist looks for two findings in the MSLT: sleep latency, which is the time it takes the patient to fall asleep (as determined by the changes in brain wave activity) after the lights are turned off, and the presence of sleep onset rapid eye movements (the onset of the dream stage of sleep within 15 minutes of the onset of sleep).

The sleep specialist looks for two findings in the MSLT:

- Sleep latency, which is the time it takes the patient to fall asleep (as determined by the changes in brain wave activity) after the lights are turned off

- The presence of sleep onset rapid eye movements (the onset of the dream stage of sleep within 15 minutes of the onset of sleep)

Mean sleep latency is then calculated from the values obtained in each nap study. Narcolepsy is strongly suspected if the mean sleep latency is less than five minutes (indicating excessive sleepiness) and if at least two sleep onset rapid eye movements occur in four or five recordings. In sleep apnea, the mean sleep latency is less than five minutes but less than two sleep onset rapid eye movements are observed in four or five nap studies. Any sleep latency of less than five minutes is considered excessive sleepiness (pathologic sleepiness). A mean sleep latency between five and ten minutes indicates mild sleepiness and one exceeding ten minutes is considered normal sleep latency.

45. I have difficulty getting to sleep and, many times, I wake up in the middle of the night. I am an anxious-type person and periodically go into a phase of depression. Can anxiety and depression cause sleep problems?

Anxiety and depression are the two most common psychiatric problems causing sleep disturbance in the general population. Anxiety is the most common psychiatric illness, followed by depression. Anxiety disorders may include generalized anxiety disorder, phobia or fear, obsessive-compulsive disorder (OCD), panic disorder, and post-traumatic stress disorder (PTSD). Insomnia is the most common sleep problem in patients with anxiety disorder. Patients present with difficulty getting to sleep and remaining asleep—they wake up repeatedly throughout the night, causing them to receive an inadequate amount of sleep.

OCD is characterized by repeated obsessions or intrusive thoughts and compulsions or repetitive compulsive behavior secondary to obsessions. In OCD patients, their obsessions and compulsions are associated with severe anxiety and sleep disturbance.

Although most panic attacks occur during the daytime, some may arise during sleep. Affected individuals wake up at night with extreme fear and anxiety, palpitation, rapid heart beat, heavy breathing, tremulousness, sweating, and fear of impending heart attacks or death. Panic attacks generally occur during the non-dream stage of sleep but sometimes may happen during the dream stage of sleep. Most patients with panic attacks complain of sleep maintenance and sleep initiation problems.

Patients with PTSD are prone to anxiety-provoking dreams and flash-backs. These episodes occur both during REM sleep (dream stage) as well as NREM sleep (non-dream stage). Post-traumatic, life-threatening, or unpleasant events (for example, torture, war, Holocaust experiences, or other physical and sexual abuse in the past) are reenacted during the dreams of PTSD patients. They suffer from chronic insomnia and are in a hyperarousal state. Some investigators consider PTSD to be a disorder of REM sleep.

Anxiety and depression sometimes coexist. Several epidemiological surveys have clearly shown an association between insomnia and depression. In addition, studies have shown that individuals with insomnia are

Anxiety and depression are the two most common psychiatric problems causing sleep disturbance in the general population.

many times more likely to develop a new psychiatric disorder—in particular, major depression within a year of the onset of insomnia and even within a year after the improvement of insomnia. Approximately 90 percent of patients with major depression or mood disorders suffer from insomnia, and a smaller percentage of patients present with excessive daytime sleepiness. A characteristic mode of presentation in depression is early morning awakening, which is more intense in older persons than it is in younger individuals. Overnight sleep studies (see question #43) in depressed individuals characteristically show early-onset dream stage (REM) sleep, maldistribution of REM cycles, increased number of eye movements during REM sleep, decreased deeper stage of sleep, and shorter total sleep time. Individuals with bipolar depression (those with up-and-down mood swings) may have excessive daytime sleepiness rather than insomnia, particularly young individuals with this disease.

Because depression and anxiety are common causes of insomnia, it is important to watch for signs of depression. These symptoms may include loss of interest in work and most activities, depressed feelings, a change in weight, sleep disturbance, reduced concentration, feelings of worthlessness, or suicidal thoughts. Immediate professional help should be sought if such symptoms are noted, as effective treatment is available.

46. I am a 30-year-old woman who has been suffering from depression for a long time. This depression is particularly notable during the winter; during the summer, I feel fine. I have terrible sleep problems during the winter. What can I do?

The symptoms described here are typical of seasonal affective depression (SAD), also known as winter depression. In this condition, symptoms of depression begin to appear in the months of October—November, when the hours of darkness (nighttime) begin to exceed the hours of light (daytime). The symptoms of depression gradually lift in the spring and summer as the days lengthen. In addition to depression in the winter, SAD-affected individuals have an excessive appetite with cravings for carbohydrates and weight gain. The condition is more common in younger women than it is in older women and more common in higher latitudes (northern climate).

You should ask your family physician to refer you to a sleep specialist, who may suggest bright light treatment for you if he or she is satisfied that you have SAD.

Many SAD patients respond to bright light exposure in the morning. You should ask your family physician to refer you to a sleep specialist, who may suggest bright light treatment for you if he or she is satisfied that you have SAD.

47. I am a 20-year-old woman. I wake up in the middle of the night to eat and drink. Is this behavior abnormal?

This patient may be suffering from nocturnal eating (drinking) syndrome. In the International Classification of Sleep Disorders, this syndrome is thought to occur more commonly in children, although some varieties of nocturnal eating or drinking syndrome affect young adults, particularly women. These individuals repeatedly wake up during the night to eat and drink, and they have insomnia. More than 50 percent of their total calories are consumed during the night. Often, they experience a craving for carbohydrates, causing weight gain. Some may have an underlying depression as well.

The treatment of nocturnal eating (drinking) syndrome consists of behavioral modification, calorie restriction, and sometimes medications such as antidepressants.

Nocturnal eating and drinking syndrome differs from bulimia, which also affects young women. In bulimia, the patient has a craving for excessive eating and drinking characterized by binge eating and often purging and vomiting. Bulimia is not restricted to the night, which differentiates it from nocturnal eating and drinking syndrome. The treatment of nocturnal eating (drinking) syndrome consists of behavioral modification, calorie restriction, and sometimes medications such as antidepressants.

48. My cousin has bipolar depression and takes a variety of medications. He is always falling asleep in the daytime. Can these medications cause sleep problems?

A variety of antidepressants are used to treat patients with bipolar depression. Some of these medications have a prolonged elimination time and, hence, persisting effects in the daytime, causing sedation and sleepiness in the daytime. In addition, some antidepressants have hypnotic properties (for example, Elavil, trazodone). These drugs are generally recommended for evening use; if they are used during the daytime, they will cause the patient to fall asleep in the daytime.

Some of these medications have a prolonged elimination time and, hence, persisting effects in the daytime, causing sedation and sleepiness in the daytime.

Most antidepressants belonging to the tricyclic group (so named because these drugs have a three-ring chemical structure) will cause daytime sleepiness and impairment of function during the daytime. Other drugs, such as Prozac and Lithium, may have alerting effects, disturbing nighttime sleep with repeated awakenings and exerting some sedative effects during the daytime.

In addition to the potential for antidepressant medications to cause excessive daytime sleepiness, the bipolar depression itself may cause excessive sleepiness during the depression phase.

49. My father has angina and heart failure. His sleep at night is very disturbed. Can it be due to heart problems?

Sleep disturbances in the form of difficulty in initiating sleep and maintaining sleep continuity are very common in a variety of medical disorders, including heart disease. Your father suffers from angina and heart failure, which often cause not only nighttime sleep disturbance but also excessive sleepiness in the daytime as a result of the disturbed and inadequate amount of sleep at night.

How does angina or heart failure cause sleep disturbance? Angina results from a narrowing of the coronary arteries (blood vessels supplying oxygen and metabolites to the heart). When angina patients exert themselves, there is a lack of blood supply to the heart relative to the demand. This imbalance causes chest pain. Sometimes the pain may awaken the patient at night—a condition known as nocturnal angina. Some patients wake up frequently at night, resulting in insufficient hours of sleep. Nocturnal angina may arise during both the dream and non-dream stages of sleep, but most often occurs during the dream stage of sleep. Many investigators have noted an association between sleep disturbances and anginal attacks. Some such patients also have sleep apnea (see question #20), which causes reduced blood oxygen saturation and thus renders them more susceptible to anginal pain.

Nocturnal angina may arise during both the dream and non-dream stages of sleep, but most often occurs during the dream stage of sleep.

In some cases, patients may experience heart attacks as a result of inadequate blood supply to a particular portion of the muscle of the heart; a small area of the muscle of the heart is then damaged, which in turn damages the heart muscle pump. These events may result in heart failure when the heart muscle cannot pump blood adequately to different body regions. The ensuing failure of many organs, including the liver, lungs, and brain, may result in shortness of breath, leg swelling, impairment of memory, difficulty sleeping at night, and excessive sleepiness in the daytime. Such patients need urgent attention from both heart and sleep specialists.

Adequate investigations and treatment for anginal pain and heart failure using drugs, oxygen inhalation, and sometimes special treatment for sleep apnea can improve the quality of life for such patients. In addition, they may prevent irregularities of heart rhythm and sudden death.

50. I have acid regurgitation, which wakes me up frequently at night, disturbing my sleep. What shall I do?

Acid regurgitation is a condition in which acid from the stomach flows back into the esophagus (the lower part of the food tube connected to the stomach) and into the mouth. The acid acts as an irritant, causing a burning sensation behind the breastbone (heartburn) and leaving a pungent, sour taste in the mouth. These symptoms frequently occur when a person is lying down in bed at night during sleep. The burning pain causes frequent awakenings, difficulty going back to sleep, and insufficient sleep. Such reflux disease is common in middle-aged and elderly people and sometimes in younger women during pregnancy.

Reflux heartburn is usually relieved by sitting up; in contrast, anginal pain is not necessarily relieved by taking such a position. When the pain travels to the neck, jaw, or left arm, anginal pain should be strongly suspected and urgent help should be sought.

The symptoms of acid reflux can be relieved by sitting up or by ingesting food or acid suppressant medications. Repeated episodes, causing inflammation of the lower esophagus, may lead to a condition that is a precursor to cancer of the esophagus. Consequently, medical advice should be sought early regarding this condition.

Sometimes acid reflux disease may cause aspiration of the stomach contents into the respiratory passages, giving rise to aspiration pneumonia (inflammation of the lungs). Nocturnal anginal pain (see question #49) may also be mistaken for heartburn. Although anginal pain generally occurs on exertion, a particular variety called nocturnal angina may be difficult to differentiate from heartburn caused by reflux disease. Reflux heartburn is usually relieved by sitting up; in contrast, anginal pain is not necessarily relieved by taking such a position. When the pain travels to the neck, jaw, or left arm, anginal pain should be strongly suspected and urgent help should be sought.

51. I have been excessively sleepy in the daytime. I wake up frequently at night. My doctor took a blood test and told me that I had low functioning of the thyroid gland. Can my excessive sleepiness be due to thyroid problems and, if so, can it be treated?

This problem may be caused by sleep apnea (see question #20), which is sometimes associated with hypofunction (that is, reduced function) of the thyroid gland (located in front of the windpipe in the neck). Normal thyroid gland function is important for body metabolism. Reduced thyroid function commonly occurs in middle-aged and elderly individuals, and it is more common in women than men. The patient may complain of fatigue and constant tiredness, weight gain, slowing down physically and mentally, dryness of the skin, sensitivity to cold temperature, constipation, sometimes anginal pain, and sleep apnea. Cessation of breathing or marked reduction of breathing during sleep in this condition may reflect deposition of fatty tissues in the region of the upper airway passage, which obstructs airflow to the lungs during sleep. In addition, hypofunction of the thyroid gland may affect regulation of the brain

It is imperative to consult your family physician as well as a sleep specialist if you have such symptoms early to avoid any serious long-term complications.

centers controlling respiration. Because of repeated apneas during sleep, the patient may wake up frequently at night, causing severe sleep disturbance. The insufficient sleep at night leads to excessive sleepiness in the daytime. This sleepiness could, of course, be related to the hypofunction of the thyroid gland only, without associated sleep apnea.

Hypofunction of the thyroid gland can be effectively treated with thyroid replacement medication. Some patients may also need a special mask treatment for sleep apnea (see question #24). Reports in the literature suggest that adequate treatment of sleep apnea can completely relieve sleep disturbance, daytime sleepiness, and other symptoms resulting from thyroid hypofunction. It is imperative to consult your family physician as well as a sleep specialist if you have such symptoms early to avoid any serious long-term complications.

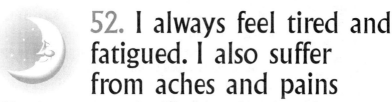 **52. I always feel tired and fatigued. I also suffer from aches and pains all over my body and certain spots are tender to touch. I have difficulty sleeping. My friend has heard of conditions called fibromyalgia and chronic fatigue syndrome. Is it possible that I have fibromyalgia or chronic fatigue syndrome, and do these conditions cause sleep disturbance?**

Both fibromyalgia and chronic fatigue syndrome can cause nighttime sleep disturbance, daytime fatigue, tiredness, and sleepiness. An estimated

3 to 6 million Americans suffer from fibromyalgia, a type of rheumatoid disease that does not affect bones or joints. Individuals suffering from this condition complain of diffuse muscle aches and pains throughout the body but most commonly in the neck, shoulders, lower back, and buttocks. No single diagnostic laboratory test can detect fibromyalgia. Instead, the condition is diagnosed based on history and physical examination, and after exclusion of other causes of muscle, bone, and joint pains. The cause of fibromyalgia remains undetermined, but many researchers are studying it in order to better understand the nature of the illness.

Sleep complaint is very common with fibromyalgia. Patients complain of repeated awakenings and decreased amount of total sleep. Sleep is not restorative or refreshing. As a result of the nighttime sleep disturbance, patients complain of daytime fatigue and sleepiness. An overnight sleep study (see question #43) may show intrusion of waking brain electrical activity into the sleep pattern, though the same findings have been noted in everal other conditions and even in some normal people. Some patients with fibromyalgia experience repeated leg jerkings during sleep at night (see question #38), which could be documented during an overnight sleep study. Sleep specialists recommend a combination of treatments for fibromyalgia: drug therapy with tricyclic antidepressants; short-term use of sleeping medications; an exercise program; education; and reassurance.

Both fibromyalgia and chronic fatigue syndrome can cause nighttime sleep disturbance, daytime fatigue, tiredness, and sleepiness.

Fibromyalgia and chronic fatigue syndrome (CFS) share some overlapping symptoms. Both conditions remain controversial and have undetermined causes. Many patients with CFS report nighttime sleep disturbance, daytime fatigue and sleepiness, similar to the symptoms noted in fibromyalgia patients. An overnight sleep study in CFS patients may show delayed sleep onset and repeated awakenings but such study has not been performed in a large number of patients. Sometimes sleep apnea and leg jerking during sleep may coexist in these patients.

The diagnosis of CFS depends on the history and the physical examination, and exclusion of other causes for the fatigue after extensive laboratory investigations. Some patients with CFS may have depression or other psychological problems. Over the years, investigators have suggested a variety of viruses as possible causes of this disease, but as yet none has been definitely associated with the condition.

An important laboratory test in CFS is recording of blood pressure and pulse rate on a tilt table, as many patients show a fall of blood pressure in the upright position, which causes fainting feelings. In such patients, drugs can be used to maintain the blood pressure while they are standing. In other patients, treatment is similar to that suggested for fibromyalgia.

53. I suffer from emphysema and chronic bronchitis. I have been experiencing sleep problems lately. Can my sleep problems be due to my lung disease?

Lung disease is an important medical cause of sleep problems. Patients with chronic bronchitis (inflammation of the lower airway passage) and emphysema (hyperinflation of the lungs) suffer from chronic cough, shortness of breath on exertion, and tightness in the chest. Listening to the chest with a stethoscope reveals many abnormalities, particularly during an acute episode, which can be confirmed by chest X rays and lung function tests in the laboratory. Air exchange occurs in the lungs during breathing to maintain normal blood oxygen levels.

Sometimes, the condition may coexist with sleep apnea. Chronic bronchitis and emphysema are serious conditions. It is advisable to consult both lung and sleep specialists so that appropriate tests may be performed to diagnose and institute optimal treatment of them.

Because of the disease affecting the lungs and the lower airways, air exchange is impaired. As a result, blood oxygen levels fall below the normal range and decline even further during sleep at night. Many patients who suffer from chronic bronchitis and long-term emphysema develop chronic heart failure and irregular heart rhythm. In these individuals, sleep disturbance may include difficulty getting to sleep and repeated awakenings throughout the night, causing insufficient sleep and daytime sleepiness. Sometimes, the condition may coexist with sleep apnea.

Chronic bronchitis and emphysema are serious conditions. It is advisable to consult both lung and sleep specialists so that appropriate tests may be performed to diagnose and institute optimal treatment of them.

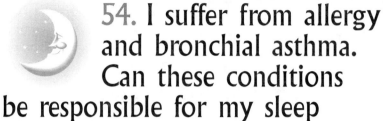

54. I suffer from allergy and bronchial asthma. Can these conditions be responsible for my sleep difficulty?

Asthma attacks may occur at any hour of the day and night, and worsening of the symptoms at night is a frequent observation in such patients. Coexisting sleep apnea is present in many affected individuals.

Bronchial asthma causes sleep disturbances (insomnia and excessive daytime sleepiness) similar to those noted in patients with emphysema and chronic bronchitis. Patients with bronchial asthma suffer from intermittent episodes of respiratory distress, wheezing, and cough. Prolonged episodes lasting for hours could be life-threatening. Asthma attacks may occur at any hour of the day and night, and worsening of the symptoms at night is a frequent observation in such patients. Coexisting sleep apnea is present in many affected individuals. Patients should consult both lung and sleep specialists for adequate investigations and treatment of their condition.

55. I have Lyme disease. Can it cause sleep disturbances?

Professional help should be sought at the slightest suspicion in the initial period, as the disease shows an excellent response to treatment with antibiotics shortly after the onset of illness following tick bites.

Although sleep complaints are common in Lyme disease, adequate studies in a large number of patients have not been conducted to fully elucidate the link between sleeping problems and this condition. Patients may experience difficulty going to sleep at night, wake up repeatedly during sleep, have insufficient hours of sleep, and suffer from daytime fatigue and sleepiness.

Lyme disease is caused by infection with an organism that is transmitted to humans by tick bites.

Shortly after the tick bite, the infected individual develops a characteristic skin rash, followed by fever, general malaise, and tiredness. Weeks to months after the initial illness, approximately 60 percent of patients will develop joint problems; in 8 to 15 percent, the nervous system and the heart may be affected. Professional help should be sought at the slightest suspicion in the initial period, as the disease shows an excellent response to treatment with antibiotics shortly after the onset of illness following tick bites.

56. I had paralytic poliomyelitis as a young adult and made a reasonably good recovery from my paralysis. Now at the age of 60, I am again experiencing weakness of my previously paralyzed leg and am also feeling some weakness in other extremities. In addition, I have aches and pains and sleep problems. Am I developing postpolio syndrome?

This patient may have postpolio syndrome. With this syndrome, there is usually a history of poliomyelitis in childhood or early adult life, accompanied by paralysis of muscles and often breathing difficulties. Years after recovering from the initial illness, the patient may visit a physician with complaints of weakness of the previously affected arm or leg plus weakness of the muscles of the other extremities. Patients also complain of aches and pains and sleep difficulty. The sleep problems may reflect the past involvement of the nerve cells in the brain controlling sleep-wake systems and breathing centers. Whether there is further involvement of the nerve cells years later remains unknown; the exact mechanism of postpolio syndrome has not yet been elucidated.

Many such patients have sleep apnea (see question #20), which can be documented only by an overnight sleep study (see question #43). As a result of repeated apneas and reduced ventilation during sleep, they may wake up frequently, causing interrupted sleep and excessive daytime sleepiness. It is important to diagnose the nature of the sleep and breathing abnormalities, because effective treatment is available. Without treatment, patients may develop adverse long-term consequences associated with sleep-related breathing disturbances (see question #22).

> *It is important to diagnose the nature of the sleep and breathing abnormalities, because effective treatment is available.*

57. My friend suffers from Lou Gehrig's disease. He is having lots of sleep and breathing difficulties. Should he see a sleep specialist?

Your friend should definitely see a sleep specialist. Lou Gehrig's disease (amyotrophic lateral sclerosis, or ALS) is a serious condition characterized by progressive death of the nerve cells controlling muscles of the body. An affected individual also suffers loss of function of the nerve cells regulating breathing. As a result, he or she develops breathing difficulties, which worsen during sleep—giving rise to sleep apnea (see question #20) and lowering of blood oxygen saturation. Sleep difficulties result from repeated episodes of apnea during sleep. Sleep is profoundly disturbed, and the patient has excessive daytime sleepiness.

> *Although no treatment can halt the progression of ALS, the patient's quality of life may be considerably improved by treating the sleeping and breathing difficulties.*

Although no treatment can halt the progression of ALS, the patient's quality of life may be considerably improved by treating the sleeping and breathing difficulties. Measures are available to assist ventilation, which will improve breathing and sleep and hence enhance daytime function. It is, therefore, important to seek the help of a sleep specialist in addition to consulting with a neurologist and a lung specialist.

58. I have been told that stroke may cause sleep disorders and sleep apnea. Is this true?

Many patients with stroke complain of sleep disruption and sleep complaints, resulting from sleep apnea and other causes. Some report insomnia with repeated awakenings during sleep at night due to associated depression; others have muscle stiffness and paralysis, which makes it difficult for the individuals to move.

An increasing body of evidence, taken from several surveys and laboratory studies, indicates that sleep apnea and stroke are intimately related. Sleep apnea may render an individual more susceptible to developing stroke, and stroke itself may make the person more susceptible to sleep apnea. Stroke and sleep apnea share some common risk factors, which should be kept in mind for preventive treatment. These risk factors include high blood pressure, heart disease, older age, obesity, smoking, and alcohol consumption.

An increasing body of evidence, taken from several surveys and laboratory studies, indicates that sleep apnea and stroke are intimately related.

Sleep apnea may adversely affect the long-term outcome in patients with stroke. It is important to make such a diagnosis because effective treatment is available for the sleep disorder, which may also decrease the risk of future stroke.

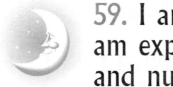

59. I am a diabetic and am experiencing tingling and numbness in my legs. My doctor told me that I have nerve disease related to uncontrollable diabetes mellitus. Can this condition be responsible for my disturbed sleep?

It is important to strictly follow the advice of a physician to keep diabetes under control so as to avoid the long-term complications of diabetic neuropathy.

Your disturbed sleep may very definitely result from nerve disease related to diabetes mellitus. Long-standing diabetes mellitus is the most common cause of disease of the nerves innervating the extremities, head, neck, and trunk. The chance of involvement of the nerves increases when the diabetes is not well controlled. Affected patients may complain of tingling and numbness, most commonly initially in the legs; advanced cases may involve the arms and other parts of the body. In addition to the sensory complaints, patients may have weakness and wasting of the muscles, particularly those in the legs below the knees bilaterally. Often, they complain of burning pain in the legs. In addition, nerves supplying the muscles of respiration may be affected, causing breathing problems that become worse during sleep.

Sleep disturbances in diabetic neuropathy (nerve involvement) are caused by a combination of factors:

- Pain associated with the nerve disease and immobility due to severe weakness of the muscles may cause difficulty getting to sleep and repeated awakenings.

- Sleep-related breathing difficulties, such as cessation of breathing or marked reduction of the volume of the air inhaled during sleep, will reduce the blood oxygen saturation and cause repeated awakenings, disturbing sleep.

- Because of the nighttime sleep disturbance, the patient may complain of excessive sleepiness during the daytime.

It is important to strictly follow the advice of a physician to keep diabetes under control so as to avoid the long-term complications of diabetic neuropathy.

60. I have Parkinson's disease and am taking medications for this condition. Lately, I have been experiencing sleep difficulties. Can my sleep problem be due to Parkinson's disease or the medications used to treat Parkinson's disease?

Investigators who have studied sleep problems in Parkinson's disease (PD) estimate that 70 to 90 percent of patients complain of sleep difficulties. These sleep problems include insomnia, excessive daytime sleepiness, abnormal movements or behavior during sleep, and, in some patients, inability to go to sleep at the right time.

Sleep problems in PD can be caused by the disease itself or by the medications used to treat this disease. Inability to turn over during the night, inability to get out of bed without help, cramps or jerks in the legs, muscle stiffness, back pain, and a desire to urinate frequently at night are some of the factors disturbing sleep in these patients. Patients may also complain of excessive daytime sleepiness, abnormal movements and noise making during the dream stage of sleep, and disturbing dreams. Some individuals may have sleep apnea with repeated awakenings and disruption of sleep. Sleep problems are more common in the advanced stage of the disease. PD patients also have an increased prevalence of depression, which may cause sleep abnormalities.

Some PD patients observe a "sleep benefit." On first waking up in the morning, they may note an improvement in muscle stiffness and tremor, both of which are common and disabling manifestations of PD. This improvement lasts, on average, an hour and a half; the mechanism underlying it is not definitely known.

Medications used to treat PD may also have adverse effects on sleep. In particular, they may give rise to abnormal movements and vivid or frightening dreams or hallucinations, which will disrupt sleep by causing repeated awakenings and arousals.

Treatment of PD does not consistently improve sleep in these patients. Some researchers report improvements in both sleep and the symptoms of PD with therapy; other reports indicate that sleep abnormalities persist.

Investigators who have studied sleep problems in Parkinson's disease (PD) estimate that 70 to 90 percent of patients complain of sleep difficulties.

An adjustment of the dose, an additional bedtime dose of an anti-parkinsonian medication, or administration of a longer-acting preparation of an anti-parkinsonian medication may sometimes alleviate the PD symptoms, though they may reappear during the middle of the night. Sometimes, a second dose of medication may be needed in the middle of the night, which may help patients with insomnia. One should be careful, however, because increasing the dose of anti-parkinsonian medications may cause hallucinations and vivid dreams, disturbing sleep. If patients suffer from abnormal movements and behavior during the dream stage of sleep, rapid eye movement behavior disorder (see question #63) should be suspected. With this condition, a small dose of benzodiazepines at bedtime will be helpful. Effective treatments are also available for hallucinations and psychotic episodes occurring at night. In those patients with repeated episodes of sleep apneas, treatment via a mask (see question #24) may prove helpful.

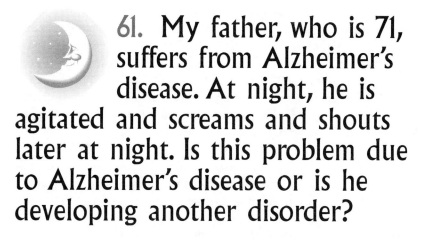

61. My father, who is 71, suffers from Alzheimer's disease. At night, he is agitated and screams and shouts later at night. Is this problem due to Alzheimer's disease or is he developing another disorder?

Alzheimer's disease is the most common cause of dementia in middle-aged to elderly individuals. It is characterized by progressive intellectual deterioration. Patients may develop agitation, hallucination, and confusion, which become worse at night. Many affected individuals suffer from severe sleep disturbances in the advanced stage of the illness.

In the patient described in the question, the nighttime agitation, screaming, and shouting most likely are related to the advanced stage of Alzheimer's disease. Many patients with this condition suffer from "sundowning," which is characterized by episodes of nocturnal confusion associated with partial or complete inversion of sleep rhythms—that is, increased wakefulness at night and sleepiness in the daytime. When the lights are turned off at night, the patient becomes fearful and agitated, and begins to scream and shout. For many of these patients, use of a night lamp may prove helpful.

Many patients with this condition suffer from "sundowning," which is characterized by episodes of nocturnal confusion associated with partial or complete inversion of sleep rhythms—that is, increased wakefulness at night and sleepiness in the daytime.

The patient described here may also be developing a condition called rapid eye movement behavior sleep disorder (see question #63). This condition, which affects many patients with Alzheimer's disease, is characterized by behavioral disturbance in the later part of the night. The sleep disturbance causing insomnia and daytime sleepiness (inversion of sleep rhythm) may reflect the involvement of the nerve cells controlling sleep-wake regulation and sleep rhythms.

Other factors linked to sleep disorders in Alzheimer's disease patients include associated depression and periodic jerking movements of the legs (periodic limb movements in sleep; see question #38). Depression is common in elderly subjects without dementia, however, and may cause sleep disturbance, which is different from the sleep dysfunction noted in patients with Alzheimer's dementia. Overnight sleep recording (see question #43) shows a characteristic pattern of early-onset dream stage of sleep and an increased number of rapid eye movements at this stage of sleep in patients with depression. These findings are quite different from the reduced rapid eye movements and reduced amount of dream stage of sleep in patients in the advanced stages of Alzheimer's disease.

Another important cause of nighttime sleep disturbance in patients with Alzheimer's disease is sleep apnea, which affects 33 to 53 percent of such individuals. Some controversy persists regarding whether sleep apnea increases with severity of the illness or its rapid progression. Sleep apnea may, of course, lower the blood oxygen levels, which in turn may cause nighttime confusion and agitation.

Other causes of sleep disturbances in patients with Alzheimer's disease may include medications that the patients have been taking and associated general medical disorders, such as heart disease or lung disease.

62. My cousin, aged 30, has been suffering from a muscle disorder since the age of 20. Now, he is always sleeping in the daytime. Can muscle disease cause sleep problems?

Muscle diseases can cause sleep problems, primarily through sleep-related breathing disorders. Although muscle diseases may be inherited, sometimes they occur without any family history. Patients complain of weakness and wasting of the muscles in the upper arms and upper legs, causing difficulty in walking, getting up from a sitting position, and raising the arms above the shoulders. Such diseases may also strike the muscles that control breathing.

Affected patients present with excessive sleepiness in the daytime as a result of repeated arousals during nighttime sleep. Because of the involvement of the muscles controlling the breathing, they stop breathing repeatedly throughout the night or their breathing is markedly reduced. As a consequence, the blood oxygen saturation level decreases and the patients repeatedly wake up throughout the night.

In such cases, it is important to direct attention to the possibility of sleep-related breathing disturbances. Strong clues include excessive daytime sleepiness and breathlessness during the waking period. An overnight sleep study (see question #43) will detect the sleep-related breathing disturbances and any fall of blood oxygen levels during sleep. It is important to diagnose these problems, as effective treatment is available—for example, assisted ventilation and breathing through a mask. The treatment can alleviate the sleep prob-

> *It is important to direct attention to the possibility of sleep-related breathing disturbances. Strong clues include excessive daytime sleepiness and breathlessness during the waking period.*

lems; prevent long-term complications such as heart failure, irregular heart rhythms, and intellectual deterioration; and improve the quality of life to a considerable extent.

63. My husband, aged 65, is a perfect gentleman in the daytime. Lately, however, he has begun to behave in an obnoxious manner in the middle to late part of the night. He will kick me, thrash about in bed, and scream loudly. Is he developing a dreadful psychiatric illness?

From the history, it does not appear that the husband is developing a psychiatric illness. A psychiatric illness will present with symptoms not just during nighttime, but also during daytime. The symptoms described here are very characteristic of a condition called rapid eye movement sleep behavior disorder (RBD). This dysfunction occurs in middle-aged to elderly people (more often in men) and affects the dream stage of sleep (REM sleep). As the dream stage of sleep is more intense and prolonged in the middle to late part of the night, the symptoms generally appear at that time.

Patients present with dream enactment behavior, suddenly dreaming as if people are chasing them; in response, they attempt to beat or kick the imaginary assailant. For example, a patient might imagine that a person is chasing him and consequently kick and thrash the bed partner lying next to him. Often, the affected individual will scream and shout, repeating the same things over and over. Sometimes, he or she may have pleasant dreams; most of the time, however, the dreams are fearful and violent in nature. On many occasions, the patient may cause injury to himself or herself as well as to the bed partner.

Taking a careful history of the episodes and particularly the timing of their occurrence at night may direct attention to the possibility of RBD in a particular patient. It is very important to consult a specialist if a suspicion of abnormal behavior in sleep at night arises. RBD can be treated effectively with a small dose of a benzodiazepine (hypnotic medication). The diagnosis must be confirmed by an overnight sleep study, using a simultaneous video recording to correlate the behavior with the sleep stages. In roughly half of all RBD patients, no cause is found. In the other half of patients, many causes are implicated, particularly neurological sources such as Parkinson's disease, Parkinson-like degenerative disease, and Alzheimer's disease. In addition, consumption of some drugs or chronic alcohol abuse may cause this type of behavior. The literature includes many reports of RBD that precedes the development of neurodegenerative diseases, such as Parkinson's disease, many years later.

> *It is very important to consult a specialist if a suspicion of abnormal behavior in sleep at night arises. RBD can be treated effectively with a small dose of a benzodiazepine (hypnotic medication).*

64. My daughter, aged 15, grinds her teeth at night. Is that normal?

Tooth grinding or tooth crunching (also known as bruxism) commonly occurs in children and young adults between the ages of 10 and 20. In the vast majority of cases, the individual is normal in all other respects. Sometimes tooth grinding is associated with malocclusion of the teeth (the upper and lower teeth do not fit well) or with disease of the temporo-mandibular joint (located in front of the earlobe). The evidence for these associations, however, is not very strong. Children with mental retardation or cerebral palsy frequently develop tooth grinding.

Bruxism involves a vigorous contraction of the muscles of the upper jaw, which rubs the upper and lower teeth against each other. Although it may occur at any stage of sleep, it most commonly takes place in the lighter stages of non-dream sleep and the dream stage of sleep. Tooth grinding produces a characteristic noise that may disturb the bed partner. Repeated episodes of tooth grinding may cause excessive tooth wear and dental decay. Sometimes the patient will complain of facial pain, headache, and pain in the region of the upper jaw. Episodes of tooth grinding are often triggered by stress, anxiety, alcohol consumption, and tooth-related diseases. Occasionally, tooth grinding runs in the family.

Episodes of tooth grinding are often triggered by stress, anxiety, alcohol consumption, and tooth-related diseases.

Tooth grinding does not require any specific treatment, other than evaluation by a dentist. In severe cases of frequent tooth grinding with evidence of wearing of the teeth, it is advisable to wear a tooth guard to protect the teeth from further damage. If the patient has a high stress or anxiety level, psychotherapy and other counseling may be needed.

65. My son, aged 10 years, wakes up approximately 45 to 60 minutes after going to sleep. He looks confused and then attempts to get out of bed, sometimes walking toward the door and going to the living room. Is sleep walking normal for his age?

Sleep walking is normal at this age. Sleep walking (also known as somnambulism) is very common in children, most frequently occurring at an age between 5 and 12 years. Sometimes, it persists into adult life. It rarely begins in adults, however. Most of the children outgrow sleep walking, with disappearance of this condition during adolescence.

A sleep walking episode occurs most commonly during the first third of the night, arising out of the deep, dreamless stage of sleep. The condition is classified as a partial arousal disorder, during which the body is apparently active but the brain is confused and only partially awakened. The subject sits up in bed, looks around vacantly, may lie down again or get out of bed, and attempts to walk toward the door. Sometimes he or she may leave the room, climb or descend stairs, and occasionally even go out the front door into the streets. On most occasions, individuals find their way around the bed and come back to bed to lie down. The subject is not aware of what is going on around him or her, but sometimes may respond to a question, albeit inappropriately. Any attempt to arouse the person fully may make the episode worse, so it is best to help the individual find the way around the bed to avoid injury from objects in the room.

Generally, sleep walking does not cause injury. Occasionally, however, the patient may trip and fall, sustaining an injury. Rarely during the episode of sleep walking, the subject may engage in violent behavior. Indeed, there have been cases of apparent homicidal incidents during somnambulistic episodes. Any such abnormal behavior during sleep walking is usually abrupt and without any apparent motivation or premeditation. The individual does not attempt to escape or cover up the action and generally has the appearance of perplexity or horror. He or she will not remember the sleep walking episodes next morning.

Most commonly, sleep walking occurs as a single episode lasting as long as ten minutes (sometimes longer). Episodes are triggered by sleep deprivation, fatigue, concurrent illness (such as fever or diseases for which sedative medications are ingested), and psychological stress. In adults with sleep walking, frequently there is a history of somnambulism. Sleep walking episodes run in the family and are often associated with sleep terror (see question #66). Occurrence of this condi-

The condition is classified as a partial arousal disorder, during which the body is apparently active but the brain is confused and only partially awakened.

tion for the first time in adults should lead to a suspicion of an underlying disease, such as sleep apnea or a neurodegenerative disease like Alzheimer's disease.

In most cases, sleep walking does not require any specific treatment other than reassurance and preventive measures. The bedroom furniture should be readjusted and any bedroom doors should be locked so that the subject cannot leave the room. Also, any hard objects lying in the bedroom should be removed to prevent injury to the individual. In severe cases involving frequent episodes of sleep walking, especially if they are associated with injuries, if the affected individual must spend time with a friend in an unfamiliar environment, then he or she can be treated temporarily with medications, such as a benzodiazepine or a tricyclic antidepressant.

66. My 12-year-old daughter falls asleep normally. Approximately 45 to 60 minutes later, she sits up in bed with a vacant and confused appearance. She then stands up in bed and screams loudly. Sometimes, she exhibits thrashing movements of her limbs. Does my daughter suffer from an epileptic seizure or an abnormal sleep disorder?

Two conditions should be considered in this case: a nocturnal epileptic seizure and night terror, an abnormal behavior occurring during the partial awakening stage. Because the two conditions may be difficult to distinguish, you should consult your family physician to seek a referral to a pediatrician or a sleep specialist for appropriate investigation and treatment.

An epileptic seizure generally lasts for a few seconds to a minute or two and is followed by a period of confusion. The episode may begin with the individual having a vacant and confused appearance but is often followed by generalized convulsive movements of the body. The seizure may be associated with incontinence of urine and tongue biting. A nocturnal seizure may occur at any time of the night and in any sleep stage, though it is most commonly observed in the dreamless stages of sleep rather than in the dreaming stage. Often, the patient gives a history of similar seizures during the daytime. In some cases, however, episodes have occurred exclusively during the night.

Night terror is a partial arousal disorder (like sleep walking) that occurs during the first third of the night. In the medical profession, night terror or sleep terror is also known as pavor nocturnus. Like sleep walking, it is common in children, occurring between the ages of 5 and 7 years. There is a high frequency of occurrence in multiple members of the same family. During the episode, the patient may sit up with a confused and frightened look and, within a short period, scream loudly with a piercing cry. He or she may begin to breathe very heavily and deeply; the patient's pulse rate may also be very rapid. Most of the time, the individual sits up or stands up in bed; sometimes, however, he or she may get out of bed and walks toward the door. The night terror episode generally lasts only a few minutes, and the patient does not recall the event the next morning.

Many affected individuals also have a history of sleep walking episodes. Indeed, the triggering factors for sleep terror are similar to those for sleep walking. Sleep terror is less common than sleep walking.

If the episodes of night terror occur infrequently and a diagnosis of nocturnal seizure has been excluded, then the only treatment required is preventive measures like those described for sleep walking. If sleep terrors occur repeatedly and if questions about the diagnosis arise, an overnight sleep study should be performed using a simultaneous video recording and multiple channels to record brain wave activities. Also, psychotherapy and stress reduction measures may be prescribed, and the patient may be administered small doses of a benzodiazepine or a tricyclic antidepressant. If nocturnal seizure disorder is strongly suspected, then in addition to the simultaneous video recording during overnight sleep study, prolonged recordings of brain wave activities may be needed during the daytime.

If sleep terrors occur repeatedly and if questions about the diagnosis arise, an overnight sleep study should be performed using a simultaneous video recording and multiple channels to record brain wave activities.

The other condition that should be considered in such cases is nightmare, which is also known as dream anxiety attack. These vivid and frightening dreams, which are mostly visual but sometimes auditory, occur during the dream stage of sleep. That is, they arise during the middle to late part of the night, when REM sleep is more intense and prolonged. Nightmares are very common. In fact, at least 50 percent of all children experience nightmares, beginning at ages 3 to 5 years. Nightmares are generally not associated with motor activities or a state of confusion. A person experiencing a nightmare may recall part of the dream the next morning.

67. I am concerned about my son, aged 1, who has head banging and rocking movements of his body during sleep. Is this an abnormal sleep disorder?

Head banging and rocking movements of the body during sleep, also called rhythmic movement disorders, most commonly occur in infants younger than 18 months of age and are occasionally associated with mental retardation. A rhythmic movement disorder can occur at any stage of sleep. It is rarely familial. This condition becomes evident during the transition between sleep and wakefulness and includes three characteristic movements: head banging with forward and backward rhythmic head movements; lateral rolling head movements; and rocking movements of the body.

Rhythmic movement disorder is a benign condition, and the patient will usually outgrow the episodes.

Rhythmic movement disorder is a benign condition, and the patient will usually outgrow the episodes. Sometimes, the episodes may be confused with seizures occurring at night. If there is any doubt about the diagnosis, professional help should be sought.

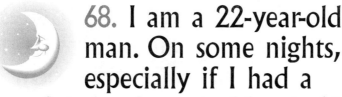

68. I am a 22-year-old man. On some nights, especially if I had a stressful day, I get sudden jerking movements of the legs with a sensation of falling as I am about to go to sleep. I am concerned about these symptoms. Am I having a nocturnal seizure or developing a serious neurological illness?

The condition described here appears to involve hypnic jerks, which are normal physiological phenomena affecting as many as 70 percent of all members of the general population. These sudden jerking movements of the legs or the whole body last for a few seconds and always occur at the moment of falling asleep. They are not accompanied by any loss of control of the urinary bladder or tongue biting. The jerking movements generally do not interfere with sleep, although sometimes repeated intense jerking movements may cause anxiety, creating difficulty in getting to sleep. Similar movements may sometimes occur after waking up in the middle of the night and going back to sleep. Again, the episodes take place at the moment of sleep onset. Occasionally, the jerking movements may be accompanied by a sensation of falling or other sensory symptoms.

The condition described here appears to involve hypnic jerks, which are normal physiological phenomena affecting as many as 70 percent of all members of the general population. These sudden jerking movements of the legs or the whole body last for a few seconds and always occur at the moment of falling asleep.

Hypnic jerks may occur following a period of stress, fatigue, or sleep deprivation. The only treatment required is an explanation with reassurance.

69. I am having episodes where I cannot move one side of my entire body, arm, or leg at sleep onset or on awakening. These episodes last only a few minutes. I am frightened. Are these events forerunners of a sinister neurological illness?

A feeling of paralysis of an arm, leg, or the entire body at sleep onset or on awakening from sleep (sleep offset) is called sleep paralysis. Such episodes usually last for one to three minutes and disappear either spontaneously or when someone touches the body. The person is usually conscious of the environment but feels very frightened and anxious.

Isolated sleep paralysis is a normal physiologic phenomenon experienced by many normal individuals without any associated disease. It also represents one of the clinical features of the narcolepsy syndrome (see question #32). Isolated sleep paralysis may affect as many as 40 to 50 percent of individuals with normal sleep at least once during one's lifetime.

The first episode of sleep paralysis usually occurs in young adults and adolescents, and the condition affects both men and women. Episodes are triggered by sleep deprivation, stress, and shift work. Occasionally, isolated sleep paralysis runs in the family. Neurological examination in persons experiencing isolated sleep paralysis will give normal results. If the affected individual has intense anxiety about the condition, however, he or she should consult a family physician, who may refer the patient to a sleep specialist. In patients with sleep paralysis associated with narcolepsy, an overnight sleep recording during an episode shows loss of tone in the muscle recordings associated with waking brain electrical activity.

Isolated sleep paralysis is a normal physiologic phenomenon experienced by many normal individuals without any associated disease. It also represents one of the clinical features of the narcolepsy syndrome.

70. Can a person remember what happens during sleep talking?

Sleep talking (also known as somniloquy) is an innocent condition in which a person makes sounds or talks during sleep without any awareness of this behavior. Sleep talking episodes may last from a few seconds to a few minutes. Most commonly, they occur in the lighter stages of dreamless sleep as well as the dream stage of sleep.

The sleep talker does not remember the speech next morning. Occasional reports have indicated that dialogue may take place between two sleepers having sleep talking episodes, though neither of the two can recall the conversation on awakening. Sleep talking generally consists of confused, incomprehensible words—one or two words or sometimes mumbled speech without clear meaning. The person may sometimes answer in an automatic manner without recalling the episode next day.

> *Sleep talking episodes may last from a few seconds to a few minutes. Most commonly, they occur in the lighter stages of dreamless sleep as well as the dream stage of sleep.*

71. I wake up with terrible leg cramps in the middle of the night. What should I do?

Most people describe leg cramps as painful, crampy sensations in the legs, usually affecting the calf muscles in the middle of the night. Colloquially, these events are described as "Charlie horse." They often cause problems with sleep maintenance and may occasionally be associated with daytime sleepiness. Episodes are more common in older individuals than in younger ones. Leg cramps are usually unilateral, affecting one leg at a time.

An occasional leg cramp at night, waking a person from sleep once in a while, may not cause much sleep disturbance or may not be associated with any significant underlying disorder. Before trying any measures to relieve the leg cramps, however, it is important to determine whether an underlying cause is present. Frequent leg cramps, occurring not only during the night but also during the daytime, may suggest that another disorder is at work. Therefore, the affected individual should consult a professional, who will try to identify the cause of this complaint. Once a cause is found, treatment should be directed at the underlying problem, which will generally relieve the leg cramps.

Sources of leg cramps may include a variety of general medical disorders (for example, kidney failure, low blood sodium and calcium, heart failure, arthritis, reduced function of the thyroid and parathyroid glands, diabetes mellitus), neurological disorders (for example, Lou Gehrig's disease, diseases of the nerves innervating the muscles in the legs, Parkinson's disease, muscle diseases), and drug-induced cramps (for example, after ingestion of lipid-lowering agents or diuretics that help produce urine). Many pregnant women also complain of cramps in the later stages of pregnancy. In addition, vigorous exercise is associated with cramps. Finally, a rare form of familial cramping exists.

Frequent leg cramps, occurring not only during the night but also during the daytime, may suggest that another disorder is at work.

When all these causes are excluded, there remains a group of individuals complaining of leg cramps at night of unknown origin. Treatment for these patients consists of both drug and nondrug therapy. Stretching and massaging the legs and bending the foot upward may help. If these nondrug treatments fail, a small dose of quinine sulfate may be administered in patients who experience disabling nocturnal cramps. Consult with a physician before using quinine, as this drug may have undesirable side effects. In any case, its use must be avoided in pregnant women and in patients with liver disease.

72. Can one perform complex acts and behave violently or even commit murder during sleep walking episodes?

Several reports of sleep-related violence, including homicide, suicide and other types of aggression, have appeared in professional journals, in print media, and on radio and television. Violent behavior during sleep is a symptom of many underlying disorders, but not by itself a disease.

The question of whether one can perform complex acts, behave violently, or even commit murder during sleep walking episodes continues to inspire heated debate. Following sleep walking episodes, subjects usually do not remember the events (except for fragments of memory of the spells) and there is no conscious wakefulness. Therefore, it has been argued that patients who experience these episodes cannot be responsible for their acts. In several court cases involving violence and homicide, in which the defense has claimed sleep walking and confusional episodes as the culprit, the verdicts have gone both for and against plaintiffs. In one case in Canada (the "Parks" case), the defendant drove 23 km, killed his mother-in-law, and attempted to kill his father-in-law. The defense argued that the plaintiff was not consciously aware of his behavior during the sleep walking episode, and he was ultimately acquitted. In another case in Pennsylvania (the "Butler, PA" case), a man who fatally shot his wife used a criminal defense of confusional arousal out of an episode of sleep apnea; he was found guilty.

> *The question of whether one can perform complex acts, behave violently, or even commit murder during sleep walking episodes continues to inspire heated debate. In several court cases involving violence and homicide, in which the defense has claimed sleep walking and confusional episodes as the culprit, the verdicts have gone both for and against plaintiffs.*

Besides sleep walking, two other conditions—confusional arousals and sleep terrors—may occur during deep dreamless sleep; complex behaviors without conscious awareness may arise out of these episodes. In addition, violent behavior may occur during the dreaming stage of sleep. It is notable that a high incidence of violent, aggressive behavior occurs in men, implying that testosterone may play a role in such cases.

Certain triggering factors may precipitate violent sleep walking episodes; it is important to remember them for the purpose of preventing such incidents. These factors include sleep deprivation, exertion, stress, and ingestion of drugs and alcohol.

In addition to arising out of deep dreamless sleep, sleep-related violent behavior and acts may occur secondary to other neurologic, primary sleep disorders and psychiatric disorders. Consequently, the diagnosis should confirm that the violent behavior arises during sleep in the absence of conscious awareness. Guidelines have been developed to identify the role played by a specific sleep disorder in violence. The sleep disorder should be diagnosed through a history or with an overnight video-polysomnographic study conducted by a sleep specialist. Each episode must generally last for a few minutes to warrant a diagnosis, and the behavior must be abrupt and without apparent motivation. Perplexity and a lack of awareness without any attempt to escape are important features on regaining consciousness. In particular, partial or complete loss of memory for the event is very characteristic of this phenomenon. A sleep walking episode generally occurs during the first third of the night and may be precipitated by the triggering factors mentioned earlier. It is also important to remember that sleep-related violence is not recurrent.

What is the basis of aggression and rage in this condition? The answer to this question remains unknown. Environmental, social, and genetic factors may all contribute to its etiology. The legal implications of the source of such behavior have been discussed and debated by the medical and legal profession without any definite conclusion.

73. Is the sleep pattern different in normal elderly people?

The sleep patterns in normal elderly people do differ from the patterns seen in younger individuals. In particular, the 24-hour sleep-wake schedule is somewhat altered in the elderly. In these individuals, there is phase advance, meaning that the elders often go to sleep early and wake up early in the morning. Night sleep is considerably decreased, and the total sleep time at night may be decreased. Because older individuals often take daytime naps, however, their total 24-hour sleep time does not appear to differ dramatically from that of young adults.

Their deep dreamless stage of sleep is shorter, whereas the lighter stage of sleep is longer. These physiological changes could reflect age-related changes in the nerve cells controlling the sleep-wake cycles and the circadian rhythm.

Elderly individuals often wake up several times during the night, including the early hours of the morning. Their deep dreamless stage of sleep is shorter, whereas the lighter stage of sleep is longer. These physiological changes could reflect age-related changes in the nerve cells controlling the sleep-wake cycles and the circadian rhythm.

74. What are some sleep problems in old age?

Sleep disturbance is more prevalent and intense in older people than it is in younger individuals. Sleep problems in old age include both normal age-related changes in sleep and their associated conditions:

- Insomnia
- Sleep apnea
- Periodic limb movements in sleep
- Sleep disturbances secondary to a variety of general medical disorders (such as lung disease, heart disease, arthritis, and other painful conditions)
- Psychiatric-psychological conditions (such as depression)
- Neurological disorders (such as Parkinson's disease, Alzheimer's disease, and other degenerative diseases of the nervous system)
- Abuse of alcohol, sedative-hypnotic drugs, and other medications
- Restless legs syndrome
- Rapid eye movement behavior disorder
- Advanced sleep phase syndrome (a disturbance of the circadian rhythm)

The prevalence of sleep apnea increases with age and is greater in men than in women. Insomnia and excessive daytime sleepiness are the two most common complaints in elderly individuals.

A careful history and physical findings followed by appropriate laboratory tests are essential to diagnosing sleep disturbance in the elderly. Many of these conditions are treatable, and treatment can greatly improve the quality of life. In addition to drug treatment, common-sense measures (see question #80) and participation in a regular exercise program are important in the treatment of sleep disturbance in the elderly.

The prevalence of sleep apnea increases with age and is greater in men than in women. Insomnia and excessive daytime sleepiness are the two most common complaints in elderly individuals.

75. Why do I feel bad for days after flying from New York City to Hong Kong and then back to New York City?

In these days of increasing jet travel that crosses several time zones (for business or pleasure), certain undesirable symptoms that constitute jet lag syndrome are commonplace. As the result of such travel, the body's internal clock becomes out of synch with the external clock in the new time zone. When the body wants to sleep, the external environment in the new time zone reminds you to stay awake. This desynchronization causes tiredness, sleepiness, general malaise, impairment of judgment and concentration, and sometimes disorientation. These symptoms, which result primarily from sleep disruption, may also be associated with gastrointestinal problems. The body's other rhythms—including those that control endocrine secretions, body temperature, and gastrointestinal motility and secretions—are affected by crossing time zones. These symptoms may last for several days, depending on the direction of travel and the number of time zones traversed. They also depend on age—elders take a longer time to readjust than younger individuals.

It takes longer to resynchronize the internal and external clocks when traveling east than when traveling west. In general, it takes approximately one and a half hours per day to readjust the internal body clock when traveling east as compared with one hour per day when traveling west. Because our body rhythm does not last exactly 24 hours (it is roughly 25 hours), it is easier to lengthen a day (for example, when traveling in a westerly direction) than to shorten a day (for example, when traveling east). When you are traveling east, your internal body clock lags behind the new local time. For example, at midnight local time in Hong Kong, the body clock in New York City will be noon; consequently, if you travel from New York to Hong Kong, you will not be ready to go to sleep at midnight in Hong Kong. After staying one to two weeks in Hong Kong on vacation or business, however, your body clock will become

As the result of such travel, the body's internal clock becomes out of synch with the external clock in the new time zone.

adjusted to Hong Kong time. Then, when you return to New York, your body clock will remain on Hong Kong time. For example, at 11:00 P.M. Hong Kong time you will be ready to go to sleep, but the local clock in New York City will read 11:00 A.M. so you must force yourself to stay awake.

In addition to the problem of disruption of synchronization between the body's inner clock and its external time cues, other factors contribute to jet lag syndrome: limited mobility while flying, dryness of the eyes on the plane, headache, fatigue, gastrointestinal disturbances, and nasal congestion.

76. Can anything be done for jet lag symptoms?

You can take several steps to minimize jet lag symptoms. You should adjust your sleep schedule to the local time on arrival, trying to stay awake during the local daytime. If you can adjust to the destination time for a few days before travel, it will help. Unfortunately, from a practical point of view, this step is rarely possible. Avoid consuming alcohol on the airplane flight; at high altitudes, effects of alcohol may be accentuated, causing sleep disturbance. Taking a sleeping pill at night during a long flight may help. You should never mix sleeping pills with alcohol, however, as this combination may prove lethal.

Exposure to light at an appropriate time might help, though the timing of the light-darkness is critical. For instance, exposure to daylight in the morning of the local time for a few hours while traveling east—to advance the internal clock—may help relieve jet lag symptoms. In the evening of the local eastern time, avoid bright light exposure (wear sunglasses or goggles). These steps should be reversed when traveling west. When traveling east, you advance your body clock; when traveling west, you delay it. It may be advisable to take a short-acting sleeping pill for the first two nights on arriving at the new destination, and after a few days you should overcome your jet lag symptoms.

Taking a sleeping pill at night during a long flight may help. You should never mix sleeping pills with alcohol, however, as this combination may prove lethal.

The role of melatonin for the treatment of jet lag symptoms remains controversial. Some advise taking 3 to 5 mg of melatonin two days before travel at bedtime of the new time zone, with treatment at bedtime continuing in the new time zone for three days. This schedule should be reversed when returning to the original time zone. In general, treatment of jet lag syndrome remains unsatisfactory.

77. All my life, I have experienced difficulty getting to sleep. I go to sleep between 3:00 and 5:00 A.M. and wake up between 10:00 A.M. and 1:00 P.M. If I have to wake up early, I cannot function adequately. Why is my sleep pattern different from that of the average person?

Delayed sleep phase syndrome (DSPS) is a condition in which the major sleep episode is delayed relative to the desired clock time. This delay makes it difficult to fall asleep and to wake up at the desired time. Patients with this problem have great difficulty in functioning properly during daytime hours, if they must awake early to go to work or school. Because of their disturbed sleep schedules, they cannot function normally in society.

The onset of DSPS generally occurs during childhood or adolescence. The condition results from an abnormality in the biological clock located in the deeper part of the brain. Some patients may also suffer from depression.

This type of sleep schedule problem can be clearly documented by keeping a sleep log for one to two weeks and by recording sleep-wake activities via an actigraph (a watch-like device that you wear on the wrist for several days; the computer chips in the device record the data that can be downloaded into a personal computer).

This type of sleep schedule problem can be clearly documented by keeping a sleep log for one to two weeks and by recording sleep-wake activities via an actigraph (a watch-like device that you wear on the wrist for several days;

the computer chips in the device record the data that can be downloaded into a personal computer). Several lines of treatment exist, including delaying sleep onset by two to three hours every day until the desired bedtime has been achieved. In addition, exposure to bright light in the morning and sometimes in combination with melatonin at night may be helpful. A sleep specialist can determine the best choice of therapy for your case.

78. Should I take over-the-counter sleeping pills for my sleeplessness?

Before seeking to self-medicate, you should find out what is causing your sleeplessness (see question #28). Sleeplessness or insomnia is not a disease, but rather a symptom in most cases. In a few patients, no definite cause can be found (idiopathic insomnia).

Before taking any over-the-counter (OTC) medications advertised as sleeping pills, you should seek professional help. Most OTC sleeping pills contain antihistamine, which is used in cold and allergy medications. Scientific studies have never definitively proved that these agents act as hypnotics (drugs that promote good sleep). OTC sleeping pills tend to cause mild drowsiness because of the antihistamine. Unfortunately, the effects spill over into the next day, leading to drowsiness, dizziness, and impairment of daytime function. The drugs also have other undesirable side effects, such as dryness of the mouth.

Before taking any over-the-counter (OTC) medications advertised as sleeping pills, you should seek professional help.

OTC drugs should be used with extreme caution in patients with glaucoma (an eye condition causing increased pressure within the eye, which may lead to blindness if left untreated). They should also be used with caution in patients who have urinary symptoms due to enlargement of the prostate gland, which is common in elderly men. OTC sleeping medications should not be consumed with alcohol as this dangerous combination may severely depress the central nervous system, leading to coma or deep unconsciousness. In patients who suffer from chronic lung disease or sleep apnea (see question #20), the pills may exacerbate their condition. The adverse effects of the OTC sleeping medications will be especially intense in the elderly because of impairment of metabolism of the drugs in old age.

79. Should I take melatonin for my sleep problem?

Melatonin is a natural hormone secreted by the pineal gland, a small gland that is located deep in the center of the brain. Melatonin secretion is activated by darkness; for this reason, it is sometimes called the "hormone of darkness." The secretion begins to rise in the evening, with the maximum secretion occurring between 3:00 and 5:00 A.M. Light suppresses melatonin secretion.

A synthetic melatonin formulation in a much greater strength than that secreted physiologically by the pineal gland is available as a nutritional supplement in the United States. Its sale is not controlled by the U.S. Food and Drug Administration (FDA), which regulates all prescription drugs in the country. The synthetic melatonin comes in various strengths, but one cannot be certain about the actual amount of melatonin content in each capsule (or whether a particular capsule actually contains any melatonin). This drug has been advertised not only as a sleeping drug, but also as a "magic bullet" capable of curing a variety of illnesses. The limited scientific studies that have been conducted to date have demonstrated that melatonin may have a mild hypnotic effect. In some studies, it has been shown to be beneficial in jet lag syndrome, sleep problems related to shift work, and some other circadian rhythm sleep disorders. Its effect on jet lag syndrome, however, remains controversial. In a small subgroup of elderly patients with complaints of insomnia, melatonin blood levels were found to be subnormal; insomnia in these individuals improved after administration of melatonin at night.

> *It should also be remembered that melatonin is a hormone, and we do not know its long-term effects on the body. Further scientific studies are needed before this drug could be recommended as a hypnotic agent. The indiscriminate use of melatonin should be discouraged until we know more about it.*

Absolutely no scientific evidence exists to prove that melatonin is useful in any other medical conditions—contrary to the claims made in magazines and on the Internet. It should also be remembered that melatonin is a hormone, and we do not know its long-term effects on the body. Further scientific studies are needed before this drug could be recommended as a hypnotic agent. The indiscriminate use of melatonin should be discouraged until we know more about it.

80. Are there any common-sense measures that I can follow for my sleep problem?

Common-sense measures consist of a set of rules intended to help you maintain a healthy sleep-wake schedule. These steps, which are also known as sleep hygiene measures, are detailed here.

Maintain a regular sleep-wake schedule during weekdays and weekends. Go to bed at a fixed time and wake up at a fixed time. Use an alarm clock if necessary.

Develop a routine for sleep preparation. Eliminate any activities that are incompatible with sleep. Restrict time in bed and go to bed only when you are sleepy. You should stay in bed for the actual sleep time plus an extra 15 to 20 minutes that may be needed to fall asleep.

Avoid napping during the daytime. Short naps, however, are good for those suffering from narcolepsy. Conversely, napping is counterproductive for those suffering from insomnia.

Do not watch television, listen to loud music, or plan the next day's activities while in bed. Do not use caffeinated beverages (coffee, tea, colas, hot chocolates) in the evening—these drinks will stimulate the arousal system. Discontinue consumption of caffeine after 4:00 P.M. (the half life of caffeine is about three hours). Avoid alcohol in the evening (no night cap). Although alcohol may help you fall asleep, declining levels of alcohol will produce withdrawal effects, causing rebound awakening and restless sleep. Alcohol reduces the dream stage of sleep and later at night may cause rebound of REM sleep, triggering nightmares as the level of alcohol falls.

Common-sense measures consist of a set of rules intended to help you maintain a healthy sleep-wake schedule. These steps, which are also known as sleep hygiene measures, are detailed here.

Do not smoke in the evening, as nicotine stimulates the central nervous system. Do not have a heavy dinner, but do not go to bed hungry. A heavy meal interferes with sleep by putting an extra strain on the digestive system. Do not wake up to snack or drink in the middle of the night, and restrict fluid intake in the evening.

Do not exercise close to bedtime. You should, however, participate in a regular exercise program, preferably five to six hours before bedtime. Do not keep the room temperature too hot or too cold. Avoid excessive noise or light in the bedroom. Do not use a too-hard or too-soft mattress.

81. I have been taking sleeping pills for months. Although they once helped me, they no longer work. Should I increase my consumption of the pills or should I try something else?

The effects of sleeping pills tend to wear off after a few weeks, as the body builds up a tolerance to the drug. Consequently, the initial dose eventually becomes ineffective. Although people have a natural tendency to increase the dose, this practice has just the opposite long-term consequence intended. That is, you may experience more sleep problems than before by increasing the dosage. If you become physically or psychologically dependent on the pills, you will require increasing doses for sleep. Over the long term, even very high doses will fail to help you sleep. In addition, these high doses may produce other side effects (for example, next-day sedation, dizziness, balance problems, impairment of judgment, forgetfulness, falls, and accidents).

If you stop taking the pills suddenly, you will have withdrawal effects. To avoid this problem, you should taper off your use of the sleeping medications gradually (no "cold turkey").

If you stop taking the pills suddenly, you will have withdrawal effects. To avoid this problem, you should taper off your use of the sleeping medications gradually (no "cold turkey").

Instead of increasing your consumption of sleeping medications, you should try nondrug treatment for your sleep problems. These measures include sleep hygiene measures (see question #80), stimulus control therapy, sleep restriction treatment, progressive relaxation, and cognitive behavioral therapy (see question #30). Your physician may refer you to a sleep specialist, who is particularly interested in nonpharmacologic therapy of insomnia. You will be instructed in all of the measures mentioned earlier. Remember, however, that these nondrug treatments may take some time to help your sleep problems and you must have patience during the therapy. The specialist may also suggest intermittent sleeping medication mixed with nonpharmacologic treatment.

82. Is it harmful if someone sleeps more than his or her usual requirement of sleep? In other words, does an excessive amount of sleep cause any adverse effects on the human mind and body?

To answer this question, you must know your normal requirement of sleep. This optimal amount of sleep will make you feel refreshed the next day so that you can function in an efficient manner. If you sleep for a shorter period than your normal requirement, you will suffer adverse consequences as a result of sleep deprivation (see question #4). If you have a primary sleep disorder, such as narcolepsy (see question #32) or sleep apnea—(see question #20), you will sleep excessively during the daytime. Short naps may be beneficial in narcolepsy, but do not help patients with sleep apnea.

One study found an increased incidence of death from coronary arterial disease, stroke, or cancer in both individuals who sleep more than ten hours and individuals who sleep less than four hours. The results of this study, however, have not been replicated.

In a normal person who sleeps for an excessive amount of time (that is, in excess of the usual requirement of night sleep), the functional capacity the next day may be reduced and work efficiency impaired. In such a case, the test for vigilance may also be impaired and reaction time prolonged the next day. In addition, the individual may suffer from poor cognition and depressed mood following an extended period of sleep. Sometimes, one may suffer from the "Rip Van Winkle effect," which is characterized by exhaustion and irritability the next day after prolonged night sleep. Thus an extended amount of sleep can have adverse effects.

Whether one can extend the amount of sleep in absence of a sleep debt remains, however, controversial.

The best advice is to restrict your sleep time to the amount that makes you feel invigorated and efficient the next day. One study found an increased incidence of death from coronary arterial disease, stroke, or cancer in both individuals who sleep more than ten hours and individuals who sleep less than four hours. The results of this study, however, have not been replicated.

83. Why do people sleep at night and not in the daytime? Does a person need to sleep at certain times of the day and night?

Sleep occurs at a particular time during 24 hours. Most of us are used to sleeping at night and waking up during the daytime. Some species (such as rats and bats) sleep during the daytime and are awake during the night; these species are called nocturnal animals.

Humans also need to rest following a period of activity. This rest-activity pattern tends to occur in cycles synchronized with fluctuations of darkness and sunlight and is a fundamental rhythmicity in all living organisms. This rhythm is controlled both by the environmental light and darkness and by an intrinsic biological clock, called a pacemaker, located in the deeper part of the brain (see question #7). Humans, animals, and plants all follow the basic rest-activity cycle, which is equivalent to the sleep-wakefulness rhythm. The rotation of the earth determines the timing of both the rest-activity cycle and the sleep-wakefulness rhythm.

In addition, the body possesses other rhythms, such as the endocrine rhythm and temperature regulation. Temperature regulation is most consistently synchronized with the sleep-wake rhythm but follows its own independent rhythm. This fact has been conclusively proved through experiments in which all external time cues (time-givers or *zeitgebers*) were removed, as in time-isolation experiments carried out in the laboratory. Under these circumstances, the body temperature rhythm dissociates from the sleep-wake rhythm and pursues its own independent rhythm.

The body temperature rhythm closely correlates with sleepiness and alertness. At sleep onset at night, body temperature begins to fall. It attains the lowest degree around 3:00 to 4:00 A.M., then begins to rise before final awakening in the early morning. The temperature continues to rise throughout the day, attaining the maximum in the evening. There is, however, a small dip in the temperature in the mid-afternoon. A high temperature favors alertness, whereas a low tem-

This rest-activity pattern tends to occur in cycles synchronized with fluctuations of darkness and sunlight and is a fundamental rhythmicity in all living organisms.

perature favors sleepiness. Hence, most humans sleep during the night and remain awake during the daytime, pattern mainly determined by the circadian rhythm (see question #7).

Another factor in the human sleep pattern is homeostasis, or the maintenance of our internal equilibrium as the body adjusts to physiological processes. Homeostasis ensures that a period of wakefulness is followed by a sleep debt and a propensity to sleep.

84. Are sleep and physical illness related? In other words, do fever and other illnesses alter sleep and, if so, what is the mechanism involved?

A clear relationship exists between physical illness and sleep. Sleep disruption is common in most medical and surgical conditions; sleep difficulty, in turn, affects these conditions adversely, interfering with the natural history and recovery process. The body's immune functions are negatively affected by sleep disruption. Consequently, our defense against infections caused by bacteria or viruses is impaired and it may take us longer to recover from disease. Sleep, therefore, may act as a host defense against disease by promoting immune functions and helping us recover from illness more rapidly. It should, how-

The body's immune functions are negatively affected by sleep disruption. Consequently, our defense against infections caused by bacteria or viruses is impaired and it may take us longer to recover from disease.

ever, be noted that the clinical consequences of sleep deprivation on immune function are very controversial.

85. Why is it bad to perform physical exercise close to bedtime? Conversely, performing yoga, meditation, or relaxation exercises close to bedtime is conducive to sleep. Why?

Physical exercise tends to increase body metabolism and body temperature, which stimulates the arousal systems (groups of nerve cells and nerve fibers in the deeper part of the brain) and interferes with the onset of sleep. Also, at the onset of sleep, body temperature falls (see questions #83 and #92); for this reason, exercise-induced rise of body temperature will interfere with sleep. Approximately five to six hours after physical exercise, however, body temperature tends to fall. Consequently, it is good to engage in physical exercise five to six hours before bedtime rather than close to bedtime.

Meditation, yoga, and other relaxation exercises tend to decrease the body metabolism, calm any anxieties or worries, and reduce any external sensory stimulation of the arousal systems. The practice of meditation first became known in ancient India circa 3000 to 4000 B.C. and was brought to the West in the latter part of the last century. It is supposed to control the mind and the body, relaxing the muscles and allaying any existing tension or anxiety. Research into meditation has been limited. Most likely, it helps a person attain a state that precedes the onset of sleep, called predormitum (see question #1). Yoga originated from meditation but focuses on a particular action, such as breathing slowly or deeply or sitting straight in a particular position with the eyes closed and with the mind relaxed. Many other relaxation exercises also help relax the mind and the body. All of these measures are conducive to sleep and have proved beneficial in many patients suffering from chronic insomnia.

At the onset of sleep, body temperature falls; for this reason, exercise-induced rise of body temperature will interfere with sleep.

86. Can medications cause excessive sleepiness or sleeplessness?

Certain medications may cause excessive daytime sleepiness, whereas others may lead to sleeplessness or insomnia.

Many drugs used to treat general medical and psychiatric illnesses may cause excessive daytime sleepiness and insomnia. For instance, antihistamines used to treat allergies and the symptoms of common colds cause daytime sleepiness, as do narcotics (for example, morphine, codeine) used to treat severe pain. Even aspirin may have a mild hypnotic effect. Likewise, certain medications used to control nausea and vomiting may cause drowsiness. All prescribed and over-the-counter (OTC) sleeping pills, of course, may cause daytime sedation and sleepiness. In addition, many antidepressants and certain drugs used to treat epilepsy may cause daytime sleepiness.

Drugs used to treat high blood pressure and heart disease (for example, beta blockers) may lead to difficulty in sleeping, repeated awakenings during sleep, and nightmares. Nightmares may also be caused by suddenly stopping medications that are REM (dream stage of sleep) suppressants; such agents are often used to treat depression and other psychiatric illnesses. Appetite suppressant drugs are stimulants and, therefore, cause insomnia. In addition, some OTC drugs used to control nasal and sinus congestion are mild stimulants and can lead to difficulty in sleeping.

> *Certain medications may cause excessive daytime sleepiness, whereas others may lead to sleeplessness or insomnia.*

87. Do night shift workers suffer from physical illness?

Approximately 5 million Americans work during some kind of night or evening shift, and many work on rotating shifts. For example, a person might work during the daytime for one week, then change to night work for the next week, then switch to daytime working hours again. With such a schedule, the internal body clock must readjust frequently. Because of these frequent readjustments, shift workers often suffer from symptoms similar to jet lag symptoms (see question #75). Symptoms they may experience include chronic fatigue, sleep disruption, and gastrointestinal symptoms, including peptic ulcer. These problems increase the chance that shift workers will become involved in traffic accidents or make errors on the job.

These problems increase the chance that shift workers will become involved in traffic accidents or make errors on the job.

Adjusting the work time schedule does not necessarily improve the symptoms experienced by shift workers. Exposure to morning light on the way home may help the biological clock set to real-world time in case of night shift workers. Although some physicians have treated these patients with melatonin, adequate scientific study has not proved yet whether this agent alters the circadian rhythm or simply acts as a mild hypnotic medication to improve sleep.

88. Why do women have sleep disturbances immediately before and after their menstrual cycles?

Menstrual sleep problems could take the form of either insomnia or excessive sleepiness. Insomnia usually occurs in the premenstrual period for about one week before menstrual bleeding. Excessive sleepiness occurs around menstrual periods. Sleep difficulty often occurs in the premenstrual phase and continues during the bleeding periods.

Sleep problems during the menstrual period may arise because of alterations in levels of the sex hormones (sex steroids). During menstrual bleeding and at the onset of menstruation, both estrogen and progesterone levels fall.

The premenstrual syndrome is characterized by symptoms including depression, anxiety, irritability, difficulty falling asleep, too much sleep, unpleasant dreams, increased awakenings, and excessive tiredness. Some authors have noted an increase in the amount of sleep and sleep disturbances in the premenstrual phase. In contrast, others have noticed increased awakenings in the premenstrual phase. Thus, the findings to date have been inconsistent.

Sleep problems during the menstrual period may arise because of alterations in levels of the sex hormones (sex steroids). During menstrual bleeding and at the onset of menstruation, both estrogen and progesterone levels fall. In contrast, following ovulation in the middle of the menstrual cycle, levels of these hormones rise. Progesterone affects temperature regulation and causes a slight rise in body temperature. This hormone has a sedative effect.

Some rare individuals have a condition called menstruation-related periodic hypersomnia, which responds to estrogen treatment. Estrogen inhibits progesterone production.

89. Why do pregnant women and women who have just given birth suffer from sleep disturbances?

Sleep disturbance during pregnancy and immediately after childbirth may be due to a variety of factors: hormonal imbalance, stress, low back pain. The exact underlying cause, however, remains unclear.

During pregnancy and for a few weeks after childbirth, repeated awakenings and inadequate amount of sleep may cause daytime tiredness and fatigue. Sleep disturbance during the first trimester of pregnancy includes excessive sleepiness due to hormonal disturbance. In addition, sleep is interrupted because of high frequency of micturition at night (resulting from the pressure of the fetus on the pregnant mother's urinary bladder). The sleep problem may somewhat improve in the middle trimester of the pregnancy. Poor sleep, however, is a common complaint in the last trimester. The growing fetus presses on the

Sleep disturbance during pregnancy and immediately after childbirth may be due to a variety of factors: hormonal imbalance, stress, low back pain.

diaphragm (the main muscle of breathing, located at the junction of the chest and abdomen) and urinary bladder, causing some breathing disturbance and frequency of micturition and resulting in sleep disturbances. Other factors causing sleep disruption in the last trimester of pregnancy include low back pain, fetal movements, heartburn, muscle cramps, and anxiety of impending delivery. Vivid dreams and nightmares may also increase during pregnancy.

Immediately after childbirth, the new mother faces an extra demand as a result of the newborn's irregular feeding and sleep-waking behavior, which causes sleep disruption in the mother. In some cases, depression at this stage may lead to further sleep disturbance.

90. Does menopause interfere with sleep and, if so, how and why?

The hormonal disturbances present during menopause cause a variety of problems. In particular, estrogen and progesterone levels are reduced. Menopausal symptoms include insomnia, hot flashes, and depression—mainly caused by the reduced amount of estrogen.

Menopausal symptoms include insomnia, hot flashes, and depression—mainly caused by the reduced amount of estrogen.

Approximately 75 percent of women experience hot flashes during menopause; these events may be accompanied by excessive sweating, anxiety, and palpitation. Such symptoms may cause repeated awakenings during sleep at night. As a result, the menopausal woman's sleep is not consolidated, causing daytime fatigue and sleepiness. Sleep disturbance in menopausal women may partly be age-related (see question #73). Because the symptoms improve on estrogen treatment, however, estrogen is likely the main factor involved.

Sleep problems in menopausal women may also follow from sleep-disordered breathing problems. The prevalence of sleep apnea in premenopausal women is much lower than that in men; after menopause, however, the prevalence in women approaches that in men. The issue of whether sleep apnea is related to estrogen deficiency remains controversial.

91. Is there a relationship between certain foods and drinks and sleep?

Sleep decreases the motility of the digestive organs. Hence, the digestive system may not be as efficient in sleep as in wakefulness, so the sleeping body may not adequately digest food. For this reason, you should avoid large helpings of spicy foods in the evening before bedtime; otherwise, sleep may be disturbed.

In addition, certain foods should be avoided at dinner. Processed foods, which contain chemical additives, may not agree with all individuals. Consumption of an excessive amount of refined carbohydrates (for example, white flour, sugar, sugar-containing foods such as chocolate, cakes) will put a strain on your stomach by filling up and overstimulating the digestive system during the process of digestion. Similarly, consumption of high-fat foods will strain the digestive system; you should, therefore, avoid eating lots of fried foods and cheeses. Some foods may interfere with sleep by overstimulating the digestive system—for example, raw vegetables, salads, and fruits. These items should be eaten in the daytime, either at lunch or breakfast.

Some have suggested that high-carbohydrate-containing foods (bread, rice, pasta) are sleep-inducing, whereas consumption of a high-protein diet promotes alertness. As yet, however, adequate scientific studies have not been conducted to fully support these claims.

Other foods are thought to have some sedative actions (for example, potatoes, pasta, rice). Foods that help produce tryptophan may help sleep—tryptophan, a serotonin precursor, modulates sleep. Foods containing this amino acid include eggs, meat, fish, bananas, peanuts, and hard cheese. Some have suggested that high-carbohydrate-containing foods (bread, rice, pasta) are sleep-inducing, whereas consumption of a high-protein diet promotes alertness. As yet, however, adequate scientific studies have not been conducted to fully support these claims.

Because of its tryptophan content, a glass of milk may promote sleep, although studies of this effect have yielded mixed findings on this point. If you are allergic to milk (that is, lactose-intolerant), avoid this beverage by all means. Avoid drinking too much liquid in the evening, as it may cause extra trips to the bathroom for urinating in the middle of the night. Avoid tea, coffee, and colas in the evening, as they contain caffeine and act as stimulants. In addition, you should avoid consumption of alcohol in the evening.

92. How does a warm bath promote a good night's sleep?

A warm bath raises the body temperature, which gradually falls within the next two to three hours. The falling phase of body temperature is associated with sleep onset. It is, therefore, recommended that you take hot baths roughly two to three hours before bedtime.

A warm bath raises the body temperature, which gradually falls within the next two to three hours. The falling phase of body temperature is associated with sleep onset.

Body temperature and sleep-wake rhythms are intimately linked. Body temperature begins to fall at the onset of sleep and reaches its lowest point during the third sleep cycle in the later part of the night. The hypothalamus (a group of nerve cells and fibers in the deeper part of the brain) regulates both body temperature and the deep dreamless stage of sleep. If the body temperature increases, the length of this sleep stage increases as well. Conversely, body temperature falls during deep dreamless sleep.

93. Why can't I use sleeping medications for sleeplessness for a long time?

Several scientific studies have shown that chronic use of sleeping medications does not help with sleeplessness. On the contrary, such use was associated with increasing harmful effects in questionnaire-based studies that followed more than 1 million participants for six years. In addition, the chances of death in chronic users of prescribed sleeping medications were found to be about three times higher than the risks faced by people not using such sleeping medications. Clearly, this finding is controversial. What is needed to settle the issue is a prospective study comparing a placebo (an inactive substance used in a control experiment to reinforce a patient's expectation of obtaining relief) with pre-scription sleeping medications.

Sleeping medications are hypnotics that can impair reaction time, daytime performance, judgment, and work efficiency, after either short- or long-term use. In elderly subjects, such hypnotic use is associated with more adverse effects than in younger individuals. In particular, older people are more likely to become injured through falls and to get involved in automobile accidents after using sleeping medications for a long time.

The chances of death in chronic users of prescribed sleeping medications were found to be about three times higher than the risks faced by people not using such sleeping medications. Clearly, this finding is controversial.

After long-term use, any sleeping medication may lose its effectiveness. There is a general tendency to increase the dose under these circumstances, but the effectiveness of the agent inevitably wanes over time. A sudden withdrawal of such medication after chronic use will cause serious withdrawal effects, such as anxiety, tremulousness, more marked insomnia, and severe impairment of performance. Addiction may be a problem with chronic use of hypnotics.

Anecdotal reports of benefits from long-term use of sleeping medications have been noted, though many of these results may reflect placebo effects. Without scientific study using both the drug and a placebo in a blinded manner, no credence can be given to such reports. In summary, long-term use of sleeping medication is not advisable for two reasons: because of the lack of clear evidence supporting the claims of beneficial effect on sleep architecture and sleep duration; and because of the drugs' tendency to produce adverse effects, including withdrawal effects, addiction, and increasing probability of mortality.

Long-term use of sleeping medication is not advisable for two reasons: because of the lack of clear evidence supporting the claims of beneficial effect on sleep architecture and sleep duration; and because of the drugs' tendency to produce adverse effects, including withdrawal effects, addiction, and increasing probability of mortality.

94. Does a relationship exist among sleep, the bed and pillows, and environmental light, sound, temperature, and humidity?

A relationship definitely exists among sleep, the bed and pillows, and environmental light, sound, temperature, and humidity. For example, if the bed is too hard or sags in the middle, sleep may be disturbed as a result of muscle aches and pains.

All kinds of pillows, including those made of wood, stone, and ceramic materials, have been described since ancient times in different cultures. Modern pillows are soft and stuffed with feathers, polyester, or foam rubber. People who suffer from allergies should avoid feather-stuffed pillows. Pillows are very personal items, and everyone has his or her favorite. The most important thing is to use a pillow that is comfortable to the neck and head. The neck should not be hyperextended or hyperflexed so as to avoid producing neck pain or, in people with disc disease in the neck, to avoid stretching the nerve roots. Instead, the neck should be in a neutral position in a straight line during sleep. Although all kinds of advertisements tout snore-preventing pillows, no rigorous scientific studies have been conducted in a large number of cases to substantiate such claims.

Light and sound are the curse of modern industrial society as far as sleep is concerned. Environmental noise, light, temperature, and humidity may all adversely affect sleep. The sensitivity to noise varies from person to person. Women are more sensitive to noise than men, and elderly people are more noise-sensitive than younger people. At the onset of sleep, environmental noise tends to stimulate our arousal system, making it difficult to fall asleep. Any sudden noise in the middle of the night will awaken most of us from sleep. A stronger noise is needed to awaken a person from the deep stage of sleep (deep dreamless sleep as well as the dreaming stage of sleep) than the lighter stages. Similarly, light and exces-

A relationship definitely exists among sleep, the bed and pillows, and environmental light, sound, temperature, and humidity.

sive humidity causing sweating will prevent a person from getting to sleep and may awaken him or her in the middle of the night.

To promote sleep, the bedroom should not have excessive noise, light, or humidity. Likewise, the temperature should not be too high or too low. High and low temperatures will affect both the quality and quantity of sleep, causing prolonged sleep latency (time it takes to fall asleep), repeated awakenings, and a reduction of deep dreamless as well as REM sleep.

95. My friend has been using herbal products for sleeplessness. Should I use alternative medicines such as ginkoba, valerian root, and other herbal products?

Herbal medicines have been used around the world throughout the ages. Examples of herbal products used to treat sleeplessness and nervous tension include valerian root, ginkoba, linden (lime flower), skull cap, and passion flower.

Many herbal products have a mild tranquilizing and sedative effect. Such products (such as valerian root and ginkoba) can be bought at health food stores without any prescription, as they are considered nutritional supplements. With chronic use, herbal products have similar effects to sleeping pills used on a long-term basis. That is, herbal products have mild sedative effects but may also cause daytime sedation; their effects will wear off after long-term use. It is also possible to become addicted to such supplements, although this has not been proven.

The problem with herbal products is that most of them did not undergo rigorous scientific study to determine their effectiveness (and, as stated previously, their effectiveness may wane over time in any event). If a person is also taking traditional medications, the herbal products could potentially interact with these drugs. A major concern is that the long-term consequences of most herbal products remain unknown.

A major concern is that the long-term consequences of most herbal products remain unknown.

Alternative therapy consists of practices that do not rely on traditional medical treatment. Although it is used as a free-standing therapy, it may sometimes be used to complement traditional medical practice. The idea is to strengthen the mind and body, which are interrelated. A tense, stressful mind will indirectly affect the physical aspects of our bodies, and physical illness in turn will affect our minds and emotions. This idea forms the principle of mind–body interaction. Alternative therapy is thought to help fight disease by strengthening the mind and relieving inner tension, however, rigorous scientific evidence is lacking. It may combine several remedies, including exercise, massage, herbal medicines, acupuncture, aromatherapy, meditation, and relaxation techniques. Massage, relaxation exercise, and meditation are, of course, very relaxing to the body and mind and often helpful in patients with chronic insomnia. Most people gain some benefit—at least initially—from alternative therapy, though the effects may not always last long.

A tense, stressful mind will indirectly affect the physical aspects of our bodies, and physical illness in turn will affect our minds and emotions. This idea forms the principle of mind–body interaction.

Before beginning any alternative therapy, you should see a sleep specialist, who will first try to find a cause for your sleep problem and suggest appropriate treatment. It is not advisable to use alternative treatment without first thoroughly understanding the source of your sleep problem, as the consequences may be serious. For example, if your excessive sleepiness results from sleep apnea, using alternative therapy instead of the traditional treatment may have disastrous consequences (see question #20). Similarly, insomnia may be caused by some underlying physical condition; therefore, finding the cause and treating it is the first step in recovery. Alternative therapy may prove useful in some cases of insomnia where no cause is found and the individual is reluctant to use traditional sleep medications for a long time.

96. As we grow older, cells in different body organs, including the brain, progressively decay. If the brain controls sleep, then why is the sleep requirement not decreased in old age?

Some controversy remains about the sleep requirement in old age. Some investigators think that older people need less sleep than younger individuals. Most sleep specialists, however, think that the total 24-hour requirement of sleep in the elders is the same as that in young persons. Older individuals may wake up repeatedly at night, resulting in a reduction in night sleep, but they often doze off during the daytime, compensating for the loss of sleep at night.

It is true that as we grow older, a progressive decay of cells occurs in different body organs, including the brain. Aging is a biologic maturation process associated with a variety of pathological changes in the central nervous system, including shrinkage and reduction of nerve cells and fibers in the brain. There is loss of some important nerve cells and fibers regulating sleep-wake rhythms in the brain stem (that part of the nervous pathway connecting the brain with the spinal cord), the hypothalamus (the group of nerve cells and fibers in the deeper part of the brain that controls both hormone secretion and the sleep-wake rhythm), and the circadian pacemaker (body clock) in the center of the brain. These changes may explain why sleep patterns are different in old age (see question #73). What determines the exact sleep requirement in humans is not known, but most likely depends on our genetic configuration. A critical mass of nerve cells and fibers is probably required to maintain the sleep-wake rhythm and the sleep

There is loss of some important nerve cells and fibers regulating sleep-wake rhythms in the brain stem (that part of the nervous pathway connecting the brain with the spinal cord), the hypothalamus (the group of nerve cells and fibers in the deeper part of the brain that controls both hormone secretion and the sleep-wake rhythm), and the circadian pacemaker (body clock) in the center of the brain. These changes may explain why sleep patterns are different in old age.

requirement. If a marked disturbance of nerve cells and fibers (as may be seen in many diseases of the nervous system) occurs in the areas responsible for sleep-wake regulation, our sleep will be disturbed. The result will be insomnia, excessive sleepiness, or alteration of the timing of sleep.

97. Does sleep disturbance affect organs in the body?

It has traditionally been said that sleep is a function of the brain and that any disturbance of sleep will solely affect the brain. Many studies have proved this point. Sleep disturbance does affect brain function, causing sleeplessness, excessive sleepiness, or abnormal timing of sleep and sometimes affecting attention, concentration, intellect, and memory.

Until very recently, however, researchers had largely neglected the effects of sleep disturbance on organs and systems of the body other than the brain. There is now a keen interest in understanding how sleep problems influence general health and other systems of the body. An important recent study has shown that chronic sleep loss has harmful effects on the metabolism of carbohydrates and hormone regulation—particularly, blood sugar, thyroid function, and cortisone secretion. These findings may have important implications for patients with diabetes mellitus, high blood pressure, and thyroid dysfunction. However, this study needs to be replicated and confirmed. Investigations of circadian rhythm disorders in shift workers in the past have clearly shown that the resulting sleep disruption has adverse effects on the digestive system, including development of stomach ulcers. Experimental sleep deprivation in humans has been shown to produce fibromyalgia-like symptoms of body aches and pains. Thus sleep disturbance may have harmful effects on other body systems in addition to brain functions.

It is clear that sleep disturbance does have harmful effects on other body systems in addition to brain functions.

98. I have heard that people often have heart attacks, stroke, or even die in their sleep during the early hours of the morning. Is this true and, if so, why?

In an important investigation analyzing the time of sudden cardiac death (related to cessation of heartbeat) in 2203 individuals, a high incidence of death was noted in the early hours of the morning. In a review of the pattern of occurrence of heart attacks and sudden cardiac deaths, another study documented a peak incidence of heart attacks in 11,633 and sudden cardiac deaths in 1981 individuals in the late part of the night and early hours of the morning.

Increased risks of heart attacks, sudden irregular heart rhythm, and stroke have been noted during the late part of the night and early morning when REM sleep (dream stage of sleep) dominates. At those times, blood pressure and heart rate are unstable and there is intermittent activation of the sympathetic division of the autonomic nervous system (the part of the nervous system controlling vital functions of the body such as circulation, respiration, and hormone secretion). The amount of blood pumped by the heart decreases during sleep, and particularly during REM sleep in the early morning hours. Oxygen saturation levels in the blood also fall maximally at this time. In addition, adhesion of the platelets (special types of blood cells) increases, narrowing the blood vessels to the brain and heart and thereby triggering blood clot formation. All of these factors predispose a person to stroke, heart attacks, sudden irregular heart rhythms, and even sudden cardiac death.

Increased risks of heart attacks, sudden irregular heart rhythm, and stroke have been noted during the late part of the night and early morning when REM sleep (dream stage of sleep) dominates.

99. Is sudden infant death syndrome (crib death) a special type of sleep-related breathing disorder?

A National Institutes of Health panel defines sudden infant death syndrome (SIDS; also known as crib death) as the sudden death of an infant younger than one year of age, for which no cause is found after a careful review of the history, an investigation of the death scene, and a complete postmortem examination. The exact cause of SIDS remains unknown. The peak age for such events is between 2 and 4 months, with a range from 1 to 12 months.

Sleep-related breathing disorder is just one suggested cause of this syndrome. The apnea (cessation of breathing) hypothesis for SIDS was first suggested in the 1970s based on the fact that some SIDS victims had a history of life-threatening apnea. After many years of investigation, however, no clear relationship between a breathing disorder and SIDS has emerged.

Epidemiological studies have suggested some risk factors for SIDS: young age of the mother, multiple pregnancies, multiple births, low socioeconomic status, male sex of the baby, low birth weight of the newborn, poor prenatal care, anemia in the mother, and use of tobacco by the mother. Most SIDS victims do not have such risk factors, however, and few have a prior history of apnea. An important factor may be immaturity of the nervous system—particularly those nerve cells and fibers that are responsible for the sleep-wakefulness cycle and the systems responsible for arousing the brain.

An important consideration that has emerged recently is the danger of accidental suffocation when the infant is sleeping in the prone position.

Infant–parent co-sleeping has been speculated to reduce the risk of SIDS. Hazards of substance and alcohol abuse by the parents must be considered when advocating co-sleeping, however.

An important consideration that has emerged recently is the danger of accidental suffocation when the infant is sleeping in the prone position. The American Academy of Pediatrics has recommended that infants be positioned on their side or in a supine position during sleep. Since these recommendations have been widely publicized, the incidence of SIDS has decreased considerably. Unfortunately, many mothers remain unaware of them and do not follow these life-saving guidelines.

100. Where can I find more information about sleep and dreams?

You can obtain essential information about sleep and sleep disorders from a number of professional and lay organizations. A number of Web sites also disseminate valuable information about sleep and sleep disorders directed specifically to the public; this information has been written by doctors. In addition, many books are devoted to sleep medicine. The sources listed here should point you in the right direction.

> *You can obtain essential information about sleep and sleep disorders from a number of professional and lay organizations.*

American Academy of Sleep Medicine (AASM)

1610 14th Street, NW

Suite 300

Rochester, MN 55901-2200

Telephone 507-287-6006

The mission of the AASM is to promote sleep disorders medicine to members of the medical and paramedical professions as well as to the public. The organization is dedicated to supporting quality care for patients with sleep disorders, providing public and professional education on the issues, and encouraging and supporting research in sleep medicine.

American Sleep Apnea Association (ASAA)

2025 Pennsylvania Avenue

Suite 905

Washington, DC 20006

Telephone 202-293-3650

The ASAA is devoted to helping patients with sleep apnea and works with a variety of support groups in the United States.

Narcolepsy Network (NN)

P.O. Box 1365

FDR Station

New York, NY 10150

Telephone 914-834-2855

The NN disseminates educational material on narcolepsy and helps develop narcolepsy support groups.

National Center for Sleep Disorders Research (NCSDR)

2 Rockledge Center

Suite 7024

6701 Rockledge Drive, MSC7920

Bethesda, MD 20892-7920

Telephone 301-435-0199

The NCSDR was established after a national commission on sleep disorders research, which was mandated by Congress, recommended in 1993 that a national center for research and education in sleep and sleep disorders be established. This center is located within the National Heart, Lung, and Blood Institute of the National Institutes of Health (NIH) in Bethesda, Maryland. It supports research, education, and training in sleep and sleep disorders for all health care professionals. The center also participates in public awareness and education campaigns about sleep disorders. It works in collaboration with several federal agencies, including the NIH, the former Alcohol, Drug Abuse, and Mental Health Administration, and the Departments of Defense, Transportation, and Veterans Affairs.

National Sleep Foundation (NSF)

729 Fifteenth Street, NW, 4th Floor

Washington, DC 20005

Telephone 202-347-3471

The NSF produces valuable brochures dealing with sleep and sleep disorders, promotes public education (particularly about driving, fatigue, and sleepiness as well as important sleep disorders), and periodically organizes Gallup polls dealing with sleep and sleep difficulties.

Restless Legs Syndrome (RLS) Foundation

4410 19th Street, NW

Suite 201

Rochester, MN 55901-6624

Telephone 507-287-6465

The RLS Foundation was established by patients suffering from RLS in 1990 and is guided by an RLS scientific advisory board and a medical advisory board. Its mission is to support patients with RLS and their families. The RLS Foundation also provides information to educate health care providers about RLS and sponsors research intended to find better treatments and, eventually, a definitive cure. Members (patients with RLS) receive newsletters with valuable information about the disease and support groups throughout the country.

Recommended Books

Carskadon M, ed. Encyclopedia of sleep and dreams. New York: MacMillan, 1993.

Chokroverty S. Companion handbook to sleep disorders medicine. Boston: Butterworth-Heinemann, 2000.

Chokroverty S, ed. Sleep disorders medicine, 2nd ed. Boston: Butterworth-Heinemann, 1999.

Recommended Web Site

yourDoctor.com

About the Author

Sudhansu Chokroverty, MD, FRCP, FACP is currently Professor of Neurology at New York Medical College, and Program Director and Associate Chairman of Neurology, Chairman of Clinical Neurophysiology, and Director, Center of Sleep Medicine at Saint Vincents Hospital and Medical Center in New York City. He was the past Chair of the Sleep Section of the American Academy of Neurology, and a member of the Advisory Board of the National Center for Sleep Disorders Research of the National Institutes of Health. He is currently on the Medical Advisory Board of the Restless Legs Syndrome Foundation, Inc. and an examiner for the American Board of Sleep Medicine. He is the founding Editor-in-Chief of the journal, *Sleep Medicine*, an international journal dealing with clinical sleep disorders. He is also the section editor of sleep disorders for the journal, *Current Treatment Options in Neurology*. He is on the editorial board of six scientific journals. He is the author or editor of six published books and four books in press, including six books dealing with sleep medicine. He has published extensively in the national and international scientific journals. He has published roughly 400 papers, abstracts and book chapters, and has made 200 presentations at national and international conferences. Dr. Chokroverty's recent research interest has focused on sleep and movement disorders, restless legs syndrome, and sleep-disordered breathing in autonomic failure and neurodegenerative disorders.

Index